PorterVision

Mind-Based Wellness & Achievement

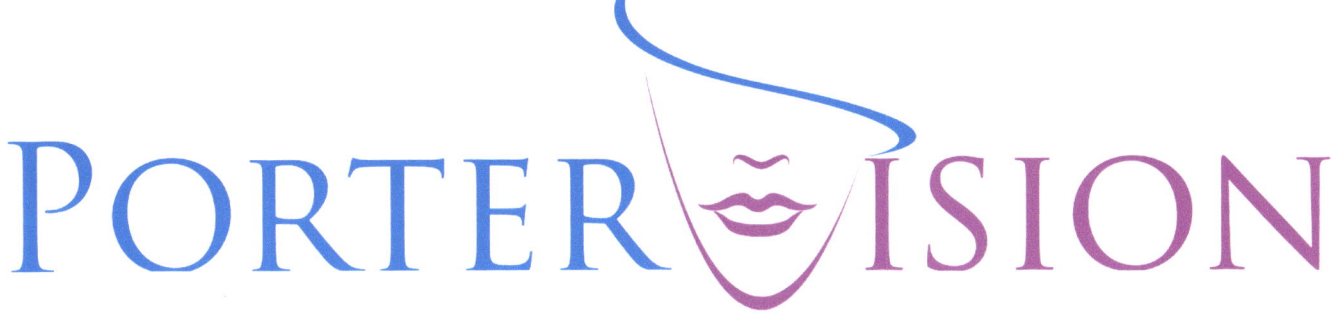

Product Catalog

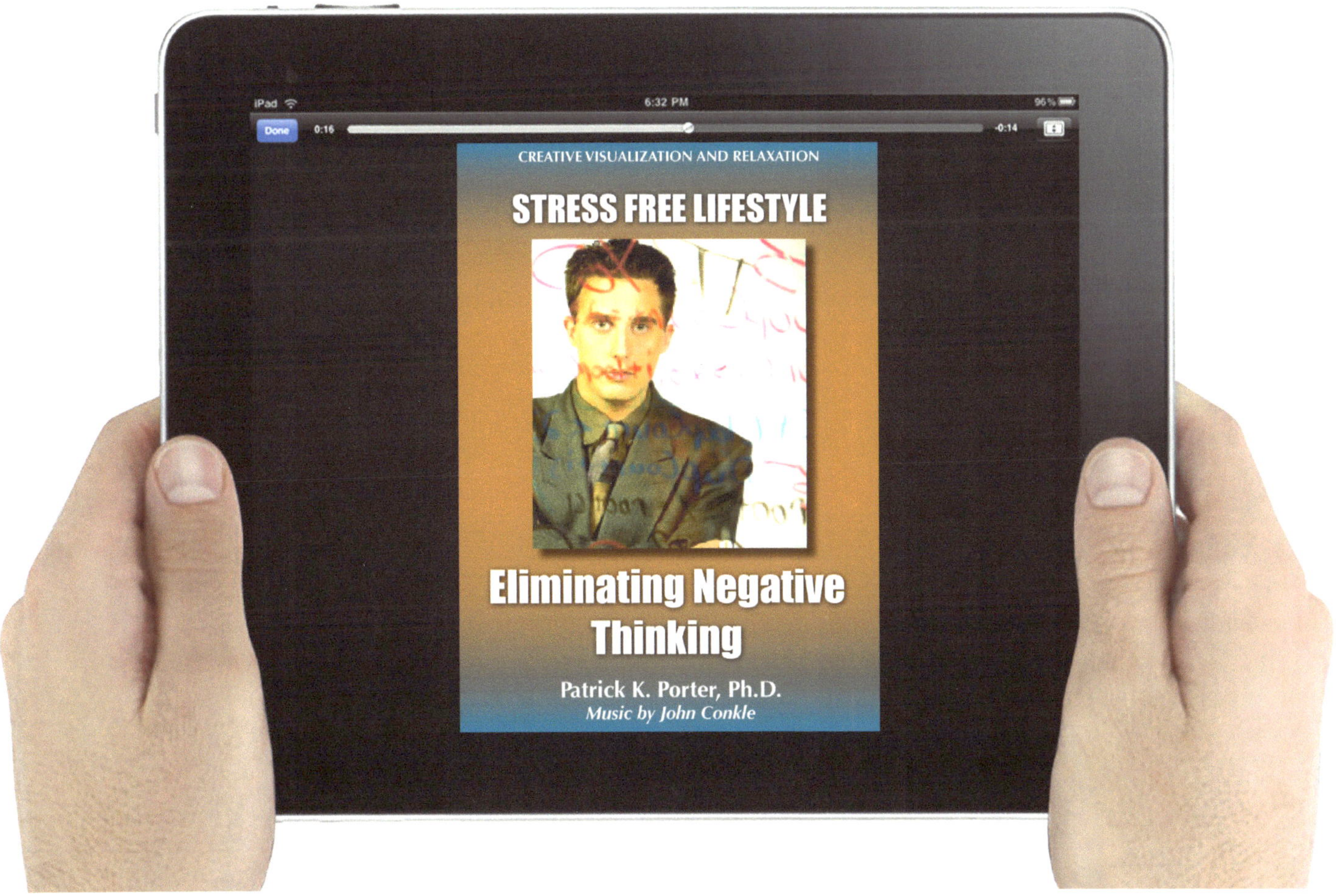

Disclaimer: This book is designed to provide information in regard to the subject matter covered. It is sold with the understanding that the publisher and author are not engaged in rendering psychological advice and the processes in this book are non-diagnostic and non-psychological. If psychological or other expert assistance is required, the services of a competent professional should be sought. The purpose of this book is to educate and entertain. Neither PorterVision, LLC, the author, or any dealer or distributor shall be liable to the purchaser or any other person or entity with respect to any liability, loss, or damage caused or alleged to be caused directly or indirectly by this book.

Copyright © 1993 by Patrick Kelly Porter, Ph.D. All rights reserved, Without Prejudice U.C.C. 1-207. No part of this publication may be reproduced or transmitted in any form or by any means, electronic or mechanical, including photocopy, recording or any information storage system now known or to be invented without permission in writing from Dr. Patrick Porter except by a reviewer who wishes to quote brief passages in connection with a review written for inclusion in a magazine, newspaper, video or broadcast. Violation is a federal crime, punishable by fine and/or imprisonment. Title 17, U.S.C. Section 104.

ISBN: 97816136404 8 7
Printed in the United States of America

PorterVision Product Resources
Table Of Contents

Accelerated Learning Series	4
Alcohol Free Series	6
Blue Chip Basketball	8
Bonus Sessions	10
Coping With Cancer Series	12
Enlightened Children's Series	14
Freedom From Addiction Series	16
Mental Coaching For Golf	18
Healing Meditations For Abuse Survivors	20
Mental Coaching for hCG Phase I & II Success	22
Insomnia Solutions Series	23
Irratable Bowel Syndrome Series	24
Life-Mastery Series	26
Medical Series	28
Mind-Over-Menopause Series	30
Pain-Free Lifestyle Series	32
Building Winning Relationships	34
Sales Mastery Series	36
Smoking Cessation Series	38
SportZone™ Series	40
Stress-Free Childbirth	42
Stress-Free Dentistry Series	44
Stress Reduction Series	45
Vibrant Health Series	47
Wealth Consciousness Series	49
Weight Loss Series	52
What the Media has to say about CVR	59
What the Research has to say about Frequency Following Response	61
ZenFrames®	65
Patrick K. Porter, Ph.D.'s Books	67
Gift of Love	70

Accelerated Learning System
Patrick K. Porter, Ph.D.

Whether you are an honor student or just having difficulty taking a test, this breakthrough learning system will help you overcome learning challenges and accelerate your current skill level. Imagine doubling your reading speed while improving your memory. Sit back, relax and allow your mind to organize your life, while you build your self-confidence and earn better grades with the PureCreations complete learning system.

ALS01 - Setting Goals for Learning Success
Dr. Porter's Pikeville College study proved that the more successful students are those who have an outcome or ultimate goal in mind. With this module you will learn the secrets of goal setting, experience a boost in motivation, and see your self-confidence in the classroom soar.

ALS02 – Being an Optimistic Thinker
Henry Ford once said, "Whether you think you can, or you think you can't, you are right." It all starts with attitude. You will be guided into the creative state, where you'll discover ways of breaking through to your optimistic mind that will help you to think, act and respond with a positive nature even during your most difficult classes or around challenging people.

ALS03 - Six Steps to Using Your Perfect Memory
Harness the natural byproduct of relaxing your mind by using the six steps that activate a perfect memory. You will discover creative ways to access and recall the information you need as you need it! Best of all, you will have this ability the rest of your life.

ALS04 - Secrets for Increasing Your Reading Speed
Our minds absorb every word on a page as soon as we scan it. This module features ways to break through the barriers that prevent you from reading at the speed and comprehension level you desire. It's simpler and easier than you think!

ALS05 - Using the Tricks of Highly Successful Students
With this creative process you will learn the best-kept secrets of successful students and how to apply them in your own life. You will soon discover that if someone else can do what you want to do, you can model what that person is doing and master it for yourself.

ALS06 - Problem Solving with Your Creative Mind
Imagine following in the footsteps of great thinkers such as Einstein, Edison and Chopin - all of whom used creative visualization to spark their imaginations. You will discover how to step into the realm of infinite possibility where imagination and creativity are limitless, and how to solve your everyday problems with solutions found in the present as well as the future.

PorterVision Product Catalog

ALS07 - Activate Your Hidden Talents

Your skills and talents go beyond your one-dimensional IQ (Intelligence Quotient). In fact there are a multitude of intelligences. Relax with this module and you will activate the different stages of intelligence within you, making you a person of intellect on multiple levels.

ALS08 - Demonstrate Self-Confidence in Learning

Concentration is key to learning. You will discover during this module a powerful concentration exercise that will unlock your true confidence. Once unlocked, you can succeed at anything you put your mind to in ways you never dreamed possible!

ALS09 - Speak with Passion and Power

You might not have been born a public speaker, but with these foolproof methods to activate your other-than-conscious mind, you will speak with passion on any topic. You will have the power and skill to speak freely, easily and clearly, whenever you're presenting, without stumbling or hesitation.

ALS10 - End Self-Sabotage at School

Imagine pulling out the roots of sabotage and planting the seeds of greatness that will help you in the classroom. With this specially designed module, you will eliminate old patterns that are holding you back. You will eliminate the time bandits and unleash your ultimate power to manifest your dreams in and out of the classroom.

ALS11 – Finishing Assignments and Projects

Imagine tapping into the unseen power of your other-than-conscious mind to get organized and efficiently complete any project. That is exactly what you will be doing with this session as you use creative visualization and relaxation to set internal time-lines and finish projects.

ALS12 - Turning Homework Procrastination into Motivation

This module will have you practicing the eight steps to transform procrastination into motivation. You will have more fun completing your homework or starting a new project than you ever dreamed possible.

ALS13 – The Power of Affirmations in the Classroom

You will discover how the right words can create a powerful mental image of you in the classroom. Let your other-than-conscious mind quickly put into motion all the right actions that will lead you to your educational goals.

Freedom From Alcohol

Patrick Porter, PhD is the creator of *Hidden Solutions*, a program offered by the Arizona Health Council to help D.U.I. offenders reclaim their lives. Now you can learn the *hidden solutions* that reside within you—solutions that can free you from your desire for alcohol for good. You'll learn to transform your alcohol addiction into something far more positive—an addiction to a healthy, balanced lifestyle. All you'll need to do is relax with these processes, which are based on Dr. Porter's personal experiences with his own addictive family and the twelve-step method that helped them heal. You'll quickly discover that the life you desire is within reach once you take control of your future—once you tune into the unlimited power that is far greater than your conscious mind.

AF01 - Breaking Beliefs and Behavioral Patterns

Alcohol is a killer addiction that is often at the core of many psychological, emotional and relationship problems. In this CVR session, Dr. Porter will guide you in evaluating the problem from the creative right side of your brain where new options can be realized and implemented. Then, with mental rehearsal, your logical left brain will show you how to use these solutions in your every day life.

AF02 - Reclaiming Your Power

The first step in AA is to admit that you are powerless over alcohol and that your life has become unmanageable. Now that you have chosen to be alcohol free, it's time to retrain your brain, which is a goal-striving organism that needs direction. You will achieve your goal by building your plan and then planning to succeed. By using this dynamic CVR process as a step-by-step guide, you will allow your other-than-conscious mind to guide you into a life where alcohol has no claim on you.

AF03 – Moving From Fear into Freedom

Every successful recovery starts with the belief that a power greater than one's conscious mind can restore sanity. As you learn to trust in this guiding force, you will release the fear and frustration of the past. From there, it becomes easy to take back your power and create a healthy lifestyle free from alcohol.

AF04 – Using the Power of Intention for a Healthy Life

Now that you have made the decision to turn your will and your life over to the care of your other-than-conscious mind, you can rid yourself of the behaviors of the past and step into the alcohol-free life you were born to live. You will discover ways to de-stress, re-focus, and enjoy life more fully each day, one day at a time.

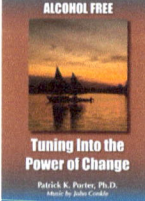

AF05 - Tuning Into the Power of Change

It has been said that those who do not learn from the past are doomed to relive it. In this process you will admit to yourself (and to other human beings) the exact nature of your wrongs. Since the brain doesn't know the difference between real or imagined, you can take this difficult step toward forgiving yourself—a step that will ultimately free you from the guilt of past behaviors.

AF06 – Gaining Freedom from Alcohol Step by Step

In previous processes you made a fearless moral inventory of yourself and your life. Now it's time to take a safe and easy step-by-step approach to freeing yourself from alcohol. The truth is that you are more capable than you think. It's now time to eliminate any negative thinking that may be keeping you tied to the debilitating effects of alcohol. Learn to forgive, forget, and move on with this unique healing process.

AF07 - Living Life Alcohol Free

Now that you have developed a powerful new mindset, you are ready to have any defects of character removed. Imagine the freedom, self-confidence, and success you will experience now that you have conquered the alcoholic behaviors of the past. Mentally rehearse living the rest of your life in health, wealth, and vitality with this calming process. It al starts with a commitment to living your life from the highest moral ground.

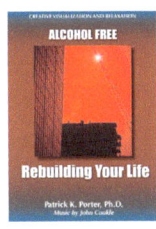

AF08 - Rebuilding Your Life

By now you have likely realized that you have always done your best given the limited knowledge you had available. The good news is, while going through this CVR series, you have been slowly and humbly removing your shortcomings. Now that you have discovered the freedom of choice, you will use this process to come to the conclusion that leading an alcohol free life will be good for you and your family. How wonderful for you to now walk tall and proud without ever again using alcohol as a crutch!

AF09 – Taking Responsibility

Use CVR to take control now so you can achieve the life of your dreams. You have within you untapped talent and skills that you have yet to realize. Dr. Porter gently guides you through this healing process of visualizing all people you have harmed, and making amends to them all. You will do this first in your mind and then, if appropriate, in the physical world.

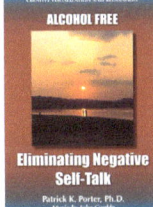

AF10- Eliminating Negative Self-Talk

You might not be able to make direct amends to all the people you have hurt; however, you can rid yourself of those harmful behaviors and step into the alcohol-free life you were born to live. Learn to de-stress, re-focus, and enjoy life more fully each day while you leave the shame and guilt of the past in the past.

AF11 - Clean and Healthy and Loving It!

Once you've made it this far, imagine how great you will feel about yourself. One day at a time you will have finally, once and for all, conquered alcohol—an impossible task made possible once you found the will to take up the challenge. This is a time for celebrating the brand new mindset you've created—one that will keep you clean and sober even in the most difficult times.

AF12 – Mind & Body Solutions Alcohol Free

As you work to create the mind-body connection of health and wellness, a deep inner knowing of your true self will develop, keeping you focused on the best outcomes for you, your body, and everyone concerned.

AF13 – Awakening to a New Reality

In this final process you will develop a deep desire for honesty along with the ability to take personal inventory and recognize when you are wrong. Now that you have had an awakening as the result of these processes, you will develop a lifelong desire to practice these principles in all your affairs. Now that you know that if the mind can conceive it, you can achieve it, the possibilities for our life are virtually limitless!

The Blue Chip Mind of Championship Basketball
With Anthony Simms & Patrick K. Porter, Ph.D.

There are two kinds of motivation that enable basketball players to achieve greatness. The first type is extrinsic motivation that comes from external influences such as coaches and piers. Athletes are extrinsically motivated to earn awards and social recognition. The second kind is intrinsic motivation, an inherent characteristic that feeds off one's inner drive to accomplish a goal.

After former Olympian and NBA player Anthony Simms experienced Dr. Patrick Porter's Creative Visualization/ Relaxation (CVR) techniques, he recognized it as a way for the youths he mentors to build the intrinsic motivation and commitment of a champion. He saw CVR as a solution for the many young competitors who could never afford a personal sports psychologist, and as a way for athletes to easily practice mental rehearsal, a proven method for improving skills and instilling muscle memory.

BCB00 -- Demo: Communication of Champions

Anthony's experience as a New York Knick gave him a unique perspective on athletic communication. With Anthony's guidance, Dr. Porter designed this program to help you experience the benefits of CVR by using the communication skills of champions. To demonstrate the power of your mind, he will guide you through a visualization for staying in the moment and a technique for alerting your teammates of your opponent's noticeable patterns. Give Anthony and Dr. Porter ten minutes and they will show you how to unleash your excellence on the court.

BCB01 -- Developing the High Values of a Champion

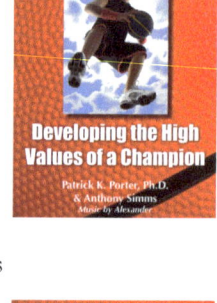

As an Olympic athlete and professional player, Anthony found that the values you have in life are the values you bring to the court. Dr. Porter will help you keep your highest values present so you stay focused and motivated. During this visualization you will be called on to reach inside to that place that makes you more. Once you see it in your mind's eye, you can experience it on the court.

BCB02 -- Reading your Opponent For Championship Play

Anthony says that in a split second you need to recognize whether the player is tall or short, left- or right-handed, fast or slow, a power or finesse player, tough or soft. During this mental training you will practice a breakthrough technique called modeling. You will set up an unconscious and automatic mental program for identifying the strengths and weaknesses of your opponents, giving you a distinct advantage on the court.

BCB03 -- Developing the Pre-Game Mind of a Champion

Have you ever wondered what goes through the mind of an NBA player? Anthony shares what he calls the "pre-game mind," or the ability to read your opponent's strengths and weaknesses and then go into battle mode. Dr. Porter has put this system into mental drills that will have you thinking positively and focus your energy toward success before you ever step on the court. The pre-game mind is a mental exercise and in it you are the superhero.

BCB04 – Developing the Post-Game Mind of a Champion

One of the biggest differences between an athlete and a champion is the "post-game mind," or the time of reflection and analysis. Dr. Porter put together a program that will provide you with the skills needed to review your performance with no regrets or judgments. The post-game mind puts you into a state of preparedness for your next game and your daily routine. The post-game mind recalls and celebrates both your brilliant plays and your small accomplishments.

BCB05 – Using the Science of Observation to Create Your Winning Skills

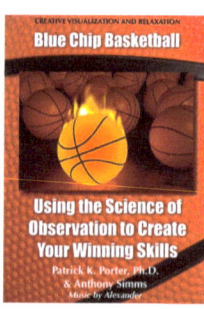

You can greatly improve your edge by understanding the dynamics of basketball movement, rotation, and direction. With Anthony's guidance, Dr. Porter created this session to help you master your understanding of rotation, arch, precision entry through the rim, and motion of release. Now when you watch great shooters, you will be in the habit of building your basketball IQ.

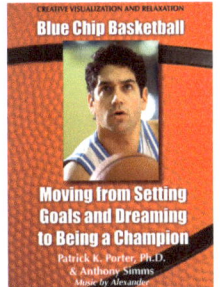

BCB06 -- Moving from Setting Goals and Dreaming to Being a Champion

When Anthony is asked what one final word a champion truly understands, that word is commitment. With mental practice comes physical excellence. You will develop the clarity about what you want to do and then you will get into a mode of making it happen. Dr. Porter will help you ignite a burning desire and an all-out laser focus on your championship goals.

BCB07 -- Moving from a Novice to a Champion with Lightning Speed

While novices focus on one aspect of their talent, champions know they must transform weaknesses into strengths. Time spent listening to this session is time spent mastering the skills of a champion from the inside out. If you learn poorly, you perform poorly; when you learn correctly, through the mind's eye, almost anything is achievable.

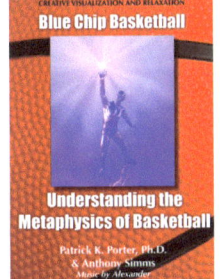

BCB08 -- Understanding the Metaphysics of Basketball

That which separates good athletes from champions is something beyond the physical. During this session, Dr. Porter will help you find that inner place where you move faster, jump higher, and meet the rim with ease. As you progress through this visualization, you will see yourself delivering offensive and defensive actions effortlessly. This skill will allow you to perform on the court with a disciplined edge that your opponents will never see coming.

BCB09 – Blue Chip Basketball

This session focuses on the mindset of the elite, blue chip athletes who repeatedly think: "I do the most productive thing at every given moment to achieve excellence." These mental exercises are to help you identify with these blue chip athletes who aspire to perform at their optimum level on and off the court each and every day. Anthony says that every athlete has brilliance inside, and with this visualization you will learn to bring radiance into your life and game.

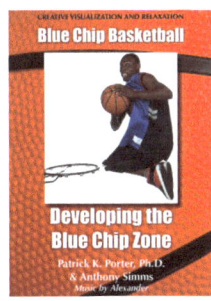

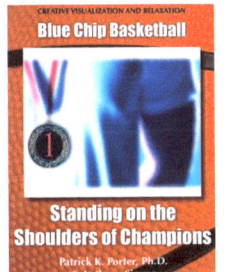

BCB10 -- Standing on the Shoulders of Champions

In this session, you will apply the science of observation. While mentally hanging out with champions, you will learn to duplicate their winning advantage. You will find yourself playing with older, more mature, and more experienced players to accelerate your decision-making and performance. You will be drawn to great coaches and absorb their philosophies and techniques. In internalizing and striving for greatness, you will find yourself humble while at the same time burning with the desire to be a champion.

BCB11 -- Commanding the Emotional Game of Basketball

Aggression, intensity, and self-control are words used to describe champions. These mental exercises will have you in command of yourself and your opponent at all times. You will become both focused and aggressive as you play. In aggressive, intense, and controlled play, your mind's thoughts are congruent with your physical actions and your skill of anticipatory thinking will alert you to what is going to happen moments ahead of the action.

BCB12 – Developing Your Coachable Mind

A champion understands that being open to new information is key to success. Anthony calls this being coachable. In this session, you will practice mental exercises to help you keep an open mind. You will let new information empower you. Your new, coachable mind will be hungry for the information that will continually raise your level of skill and achievement. Your coachable mindset consists of not only being able to stay mentally hungry and alert, but also having the ability to learn from the different skill sets that yield success.

BCB13 – Activating Laser Focus

Focus is the laser-like appreciation of the next task to be accomplished. Dr. Porter will teach to have laser-like focus so you stay in the zone and everything works. You will practice focus in a new way and will develop your own activities that trigger the focus response. Focus allows your conscious competence to advance to unconscious competence—the place where the zone is your automatic state of being.

PorterVision's Product Resources

ZenFrames Demo

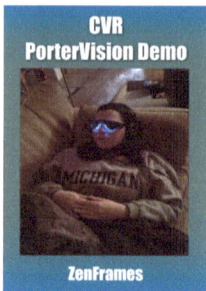

The ZenFrame light and sound technology must be experienced to be understood. In Dr. Patrick Porter's own words, "Trying to tell someone what it's like to experience the system is like trying to describe atmosphere to a fish." In this ten-minute demo, you will be introduced to the four major brainwave frequencies and find out how the ZenFrames guide you to the two most beneficial of them. You will even practice using visualization and will experience a mental vacation to your personal place of relaxation. Once you have completed the session, we're sure you'll agree that learning to use your mind is one of the most powerful steps you can take toward improving your life.

AM Concentration

This session has been designed to boost your self-esteem. A key benefit of creative visualization and relaxation is to help you improve your self belief. With this morning program taking ten minutes you will visualize achieving your daily goals, and at the same time enjoy greater focus and concentration.

AM Focus

Dr. Porter has designed this process to provide the mental clarity necessary to begin the day with focus. Our lives are typically filled with distractions, and spending these ten short minutes upon awaking is a great way help put ourselves in the proper mind-set to easily deal with such distractions, while staying on course to achieve our objectives for the day.

AM Motivation

Today is the day you can take back control of your feelings so you can enjoy greater focus and concentration and that means the motivation to get things done. With this 10 minute motivation session you will change procrastination into that confident person you desire to be. Each of the AM programs are designed to help you become successful and enjoy greater focus and concentration.

PM Creating Your Success Time-line

Imagine drifting off into a deeply rejuvenating sleep while the most powerful computer on earth continues to plan a time-line for success. This is exactly what Dr. Porter has created in this program. You will be guided into restful sleep while your powerful mind plans success in your daily life.

PM Focus In Dreamtime

Sleep often eludes us when our minds are cluttered with leftovers from the day's events. Dr. Porter created this program to help us enter into the deepest level of sleep by putting today's activities into perspective.

PM Release Negativity

With this session you will train the brain to shut off the stress and negativity of the day and drift off into a deeply relaxing state of sleep where you focus on the positive and eliminate the negative. The results will have you awakening with more energy and motivation to accomplish any task during the following day.

10 Minute "ZenSync Meditations"
15 Minute "ZenSync Meditations"
20 Minute "ZenSync Meditations"
25 Minute "ZenSync Meditations"

Ancient wisdom tells us that "our needs are few and our wants are many." At time you might want to just contemplate with the alpha music and the light and sound technology guiding you into that "Zen" state of mind. Whether you have 10 minutes or 25 we have provided you with conscious choices, and free thinking in a consumer-driven world to create your own mental vacation.

PorterVision's Product Resources

Coping With Cancer Series
Patrick K. Porter, Ph.D.

Being diagnosed with cancer is in itself a stressful event—so stressful it can suppress your immune system and worsen the side-effects of treatment. Fortunately, through guided relaxation, you can let go of your fear and anxiety, and take charge of your recovery. Creative visualization can help you regain an optimistic attitude, spark your immune system, and maximize your medical treatment. If you are ready to join the ranks of people who have discovered the mind/body connection and its healing potential, then the Coping With Cancer Series is definitely for you!

CWC01 - Relaxation For Inner Healing

For some people, relaxing while facing a serious illness may seem like an impossible task. In this first session, you will begin by simply clearing your mind of all negative or fear-based thoughts concerning your condition. At the same time, you will learn to allow the natural healing power of your body to take over. The benefits from relaxation are immeasurable when it comes to fighting cancer. Dr. Patrick Porter will gently guide you through the first of many creative visualization sessions, which will build for you a strong foundation for using the science of relaxation as a natural part of your cancer treatment and recovery.

CWC02 - Rejuvenate Your Body Through Deep Delta Sleep

During cancer recovery, many people have difficulty falling asleep or they may awaken in the middle of the night and struggle to get back to sleep. Your body naturally recharges and rejuvenates during sleep, which means a good night's rest is key to your recovery. This imagery will show you new ways to get maximum benefit from sleep. You'll start by releasing any negative emotions you may have about cancer. Any anger or fear that may be interrupting your sleep will be cleared from your mind. You will also learn a simple method for returning to sleep if you should awaken during the night. Sit back, relax, put an end to nighttime restlessness, and get the healing, rejuvenating sleep your body needs.

CWC03 – The Power of Optimistic Planning

Your thoughts continually influence your brain to create either negative or positive states. Now you can gain control over your thoughts. You will learn to eliminate the emotions that feed cancer and to inspire the positive emotions that create an optimum healing environment. Through relaxation and guided imagery, you will awaken to the healing benefits of thinking positively even in negative situations.

CWC04 – Eliminate Harmful Habits for Health and Wellness

With this process you will experience even deeper levels of relaxation so the true healing nature of your body can go to work creating the health you desire. You will discover techniques for eliminating emotional turmoil that might have you hanging on to negative habits and patterns. Perhaps a part of you wants to get well, while another part wants to deny the disease or is resisting giving up harmful habits. Now you can gain new life skills that will give you the best possible chance for beating cancer for good.

CWC05 – Tapping Into Your Internal Pharmacy

Science has proven that your brain can release over 30,000 different neuron-chemicals with a simple thought. Dr. Patrick Porter will help you discover powerful ways to organize experiences so that the negativity associated with cancer is minimized and you can relax and enjoy your time with family and friends. Negative emotions such as fear, frustration, and anger, along with physical pain, nausea, and fatigue, can limit your ability to relax and heal. Now you can use creative visualization and relaxation and your mind's resources—your internal pharmacy—to go with the flow, relax, and set a course for healing and wellbeing. From this relaxed state of mind, your body can best respond to the treatment you and your health care professionals have chosen.

CWC06 – Focus on Health & Maximize Your Support Network

A diagnosis of cancer can feel like a lonely place, but it doesn't have to be. During this process, you will use creative visualization to imagine your body absorbing the prayers and well wishes sent from friends and loved ones. You will see yourself in a beautiful field of flowers where you learn to tap into your "circle of power." While there, you will make the commitment to become your own health advocate, and you will make decisions about how to best work with your health care professionals. You will learn to ask for any physical or emotional assistance you may need, and will be encouraged to do what you can to aid your recovery, such as taking walks or attending yoga classes. You will gain freedom by being honest with yourself. At the same time, you will develop a team attitude, so you are comfortable in accepting the support offered you. Most importantly, you will develop the courage to be realistic with your support network, so you can get the help you need when you need it.

PorterVision Product Catalog

CWC07 - Transform Negative Thinking Into Positive Motivation

After your cancer diagnosis, you will quickly discover that life goes on; Work, bills, and daily chores don't go away. With this process you will put the external worries, such as money and housework, into proper perspective. You will learn about thoughts that harm and thoughts that heal, so you can focus your mind on the healing thoughts. This is what separates those who struggle with treatment from those who seem to flow through it without difficulty. There is an opportunity for you to not only survive, but also thrive—and it exists in your own mind. Sit back, relax, and benefit from the stress-reducing methods that can give you inner strength and the determination to succeed with your treatment plan.

CWC08 – Build Your Own Internal Support System

No one plans on getting cancer. Consequently, most people feel lost or helpless after hearing their diagnosis. This is why you need uncommon resources for these uncommon times. Dr. Patrick Porter will help you build your own internal support system. With creative visualization and relaxation, you will learn to use your mind, the most powerful computer on earth, to regain your equanimity. Your mind has the capacity for virtually limitless problem solving. Now you can transform any negative emotional states associated with your treatment into positive actions for helping you recover your health and your emotional wellbeing.

CWC09 – Turn on the Power of Faith through Imagery

The power of faith, prayer, and imagery has been recognized in medical circles for decades. Now you can do what the most successful patients do to get maximum results from their medical treatment. You will learn how to call upon that higher power to help visualize and realize the healing potential of your mind. During this creative visualization, you will call upon this higher intelligence to help stimulate the white marker cells to do what they do best, seek out and destroy foreign agents in the body. At the same time, you will be training your brain to think differently about your role in recovery, helping you to take an active role in working with the amazing healing ability that comes with faith and acceptance.

CWC10 - Using Goal Programming & Positive Expectancy

The mind is a goal striving mechanism. During this creative visualization session you will set a goal for creating a healing environment within your body. You will then let your other-than-conscious mind take over. Positive expectancy will help you through challenges and give you the assertiveness you need to be your own best caregiver. You will make your health your top priority, making sure your medicine is in order and that you are keeping your appointments. Setting healthy goals such as exercising, eating properly, and getting sufficient rest will keep you on the path to recovery and will make the process more pleasant for you and your loved ones.

CWC11 – Making Health a Priority and Staying Focused on Wellness

Dr. Patrick Porter realizes that you have one primary goal—freedom from cancer. During this visualization, he will help you focus on everything you can do to reach that outcome. He will help you build a positive attitude, gain the motivation to consume healing foods, to exercise regularly, and to feel that you are in harmony with your chemotherapy, radiation, or other treatments. During this healing journey, you will start with a deep relaxation and guided visualization to uncover your deepest desires and values. From there you will focus your mind on purity of thought and the realization of your goal.

CWC12 – Supercharge Your Immune System

The "relaxation response" is the key to the powerful release of the natural healing forces of the brain and body. During this visualization, you will use your creative mind to stimulate your immune system and visualize it eradicating any diseased cells in your body. Dr. Patrick Porter will help you create empowering thoughts about your immune system and then set the immune system to the task of destroying the diseased cells. You will discover why thoughts are more powerful than things… because thoughts create things—and the thing you will be thinking about is radiant health!

CWC13 – Relax & Let It Be

During this visualization you will learn the secret of forgiveness and grace. It is human nature to try to control everything—from family to friends to the health care system. This is the type of stress your body doesn't need during your treatment. Dr. Patrick Porter will train you to use an easy trigger that will allow you to "let it be" when it's appropriate. He will help you move into a state of calm relaxation even around the most difficult people or under the most stressful circumstances.

PorterVision's Product Resources

Enlightened Children's Series

Seven-year-old Marina Mulac and five-year-old Morgan Mulac, who have come to be known as the world's youngest marketers, were the inspiration behind this *Enlightened Children's Series*. When they met Dr. Patrick Porter, they had one question for him: *Why had he created so many great visualizations for grown ups and nothing for kids?*

Dr. Porter told the two little entrepreneurs that if they put on their thinking caps and helped him design a program for kids, together they could help children from around the globe to use their imaginative minds to become better people and help improve the world. Together, Marina, Morgan, and Dr. Patrick Porter put together this series that uses guided imagery, storytelling, and positive affirmations to help children see the world as a peaceful and harmonious place where everyone can win. If your goal is to develop a happy, healthy *child of influence* in our rapidly changing world, this series is a must-have for your child.

ESC01 Building Optimism in Your Children

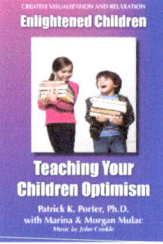

Every day your child is forming his or her view of the world based on life experiences. Now is the time to help your child build a positive outlook that will serve him or her for a lifetime. Optimists believe that people and events are inherently good and that most situations work out for the best. Dr. Porter will show your child how to see the good in every situation and how to be open to experiencing new things.

ESC02 Developing Honesty as a Habit

With the influence of video games, movies, and television, it may sometimes be hard for children to identify true honesty. Dr. Porter will help your child realize that honesty is a way of communicating and acting truthfully in relation to the situations your child is in. This includes how he or she listens, speaks, and behaves around others.

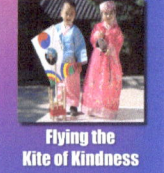

ESC03 Flying the Kite of Kindness

With this guided imagery your child will go to an imaginary park to fly a kite. While the wind takes hold of the kite, the child learns why kindness is a virtue and how to let his or her innate kindness shine for all to see. By the time your child has finished flying the kite, he or she will understand that kindness reaps the reward of kindness in return.

ECS04 Playing the Change Game

Today's children live in a world that is changing daily. How well children learn to adapt to change will have a direct influence on his or her ability to cope with the stresses of our modern world. In this visualization your child will come to understand change as a natural part of life and will learn the skills to master it.

ECS05 Nurturing a Love of Learning

With distractions such as video games and hundreds of television channels to choose from, it's no wonder children get easily bored in a learning environment. During this guided imagery session your child will plant the seeds of curiosity that will develop into an excitement about learning new things.

ECS06 Making Exercise Fun

America has become a sedentary fast food nation. Consequently, the childhood obesity rate is soaring and along with it a plethora of weight-related health problems. It is the intention of this visualization to build a strong desire in your child to be physically active every day. When exercise becomes a way of life for your child, he or she will never have to endure the embarrassment and health risks associated with excess weight.

ECS07 Practicing Patience

Patience involves endurance during challenging situations; it means persevering in the face of delay and remaining calm while in the throes of provocation. Patience refers to the character trait of steadfastness. Wanting everything right now is a very real trait of the child in each of us. This session will help your child discover that life unfolds over time and that their needs are met when the time is right.

ESC08 Visualize Peace in the World

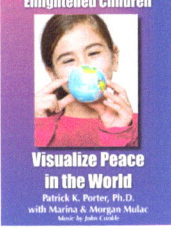

The annual World Healing Day movement that started on December 31, 1986 at Noon Greenwich time has impacted thousands of lives for more than two decades. To further that directive, Dr. Porter has created this visualization where your child envisions the peace he or she wants to see in the world by developing that peace within.

ESC09 Respecting Yourself Respecting Others

During this visualization your child will gain a sense of self-worth and develop the ability to see that worth in others. Every child is special and is imbued with unique talents and attributes. Through this process children learn to enjoy sharing their special gifts with the world.

ESC10 Being the Light of Leadership

Helping your child to become a leader instead of a follower is so important in today's rapidly advancing society. In this process Dr. Porter, with the help of Marina and Morgan, will help your child develop the ability to have a positive influence on others. This skill will help your child enlist the aid and support of others for accomplishing goals and will create an inner vision wherein he or she stays true to healthy and positive values.

ESC11 Bringing Compassion to the World

In this visualization Dr. Porter will help your child understand one of the greatest virtues —compassion. As your child comes to understand this profound human emotion, he or she will become motivated to take action and make a difference. Compassion is often the key component to altruism and is embodied by the golden rule: Do unto others as you would have done to you.

ESC12 Being the Gift of Love

One of Dr. Porter's mentors, Dr. Jerry DeShazo, was inspired to share The Gift of Love with the world. This is a spiritual poem that can be read at http://www.theGiftofLove.com. Your child will learn this powerful visualization so that he or she can embody that gift in every word and deed.

ESC13 Building Healthy Relationships

This session focuses on the basic components of healthy relationships: expectations and communication. In this session your child will learn to identify with healthy relationships and will build that expectancy into developing healthy friendships. It is also designed to open communication between you and your child.

Marina & Morgan Mulac

In 2007, at the ages of 4 and 6, Marina Mulac and Morgan Mulac became the youngest marketers to ever grace the World Internet Main Event Stage in San Francisco, California when they were invited to report the results of their www.MommysBirthday.com fire sale, which grossed an unprecedented $8200.00 in one week for the two mini marketers. Quickly realizing the power of the Internet to touch lives, they are following in their parents footsteps and as a family they travel the U.S. speaking at marketing and motivational seminars while enjoying the home school lifestyle. Teaming up with Dr. Porter, their goal with the "Enlightened Children's Series" is to help children from around the globe to use their imaginative minds to become better people and help improve the world.

Freedom From Addiction
Patrick K. Porter, Ph.D.

Addiction comes in many forms, but the underlying cause remains the same. For every addiction there is an underlying *positive intention* that the mind is trying to fulfill. Now you can use the power of your mind—through *creative visualization and relaxation* (CVR)—to find more appropriate ways to satisfy that positive intention without the destructive behaviors of the past. Dr. Patrick Porter's ground-breaking CVR program for overcoming addiction can work for just about any addiction including the following:

- Alcoholism
- Anorexia
- Bulimia
- Codependency
- Gambling
- Marijuana
- Narcotics
- Prescription Drugs
- Overeating
- Overspending
- Pornography
- Self-Injury

FA01 – Personal Responsibility
Working With Your Other-Than-Conscious Mind to Manage Your Life

Most people who struggle with addictions have, in reality, simply lost their power of choice. Dr. Patrick Porter (PhD) will help you discover why trying to force a change with willpower only perpetuates the problem and how visualization is what will lead you to realization and freedom. You will discover how, by tapping into the power of your mind, you can rebuild your confidence (even in uncertain times) and bring into your consciousness (with sufficient force) the appropriate memories and choices that will lead you to living an addiction-free life—which is your birthright.

FA02 – Tapping Into a Power Greater Than You to Restore Sanity to Your Life

With years of clinical experience, Dr. Patrick Porter has found that those who are willing to turn over their addiction to a greater power find the transition to addiction-free behavior easier, and they are far more likely to achieve lasting results. It has been repeatedly proven that, upon a simple cornerstone of faith, a spiritual structure of strength and resolve can be built. During this process, you will use your own concept of this *higher power* to reframe your past, and you will start today to live the life you were born to live.

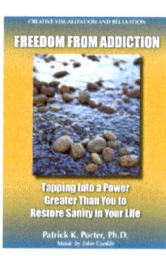

FA03 - Release Your Past and Embrace the Power of Change

In this process you will mentally make a decision to turn your will and your future over to the care of the creator, as you understand that creative force to be. During this visualization, you will release the bondage of the past so that this force for good may better do its will. By planning one day at a time, you will find that your challenges and stressors fall away as you create daily victories over them. Relax and bear witness to the flow of life, and it will help you tap into its power, love, and grace; your addiction-free new way of life will be the natural by-product.

FA04 – Taking a Fearless Moral Inventory

Every behavior, even those that are negative, has a positive underlying intent. Dr. Patrick Porter will guide you through the process of discovering your positive intention and developing more appropriate ways of meeting it. You will experience a mental cleansing as you realize that, in the past, you did the very best you could with the information you had at the time. Today you will open to the truth about who you are and experience the release that comes when you forgive yourself. Once you search out your flaws, you can make a daily plan for avoiding what in the past caused your failure. You will soon be embracing your life free from addiction.

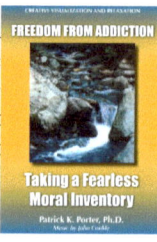

FA05 – Developing the Courage to Express and Release the Past

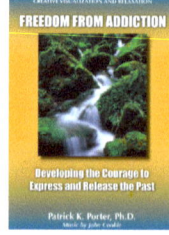

During this powerful visualization, you will gain the courage to express your regret to those you have wronged in the past. Even though this is perhaps the most difficult step, it is also the most liberating. No one likes to discuss defects with others; however, this is exactly what's needed to create the new state of balance in your life. This session will also take you through a visualization where you can communicate your request for forgiveness to those who are no longer in your life or are deceased. Dr. Porter will help you to rediscover the balance within yourself as you take this important step in the mental healing process.

FA06 – Discovering the Positive Intent Behind Old Behaviors

It is human nature to stay attached to old habits even when those habits are no longer working. Fortunately, once you uncover the underlying positive intention behind the old behaviors, you can easily learn to meet those needs with new, more appropriate habits. Dr. Porter will guide you through this inner battle between old habits and new behaviors, and you will come out the other side with positive new insights. You will release the emotional pain of the past and create the balance essential to making changes in your life one day at a time.

FA07 – Humility—Your Key To Lasting Change

Cultivating humility, along with letting your greater power work in your life, is perhaps the least discussed in addiction recovery groups, yet it is probably the most potent as it relates to lasting life changes. Humility embodies the miracle of transformation, and all it takes is turning over to your higher power the old unhealthy thinking patterns. After all, it was your best thinking that brought you to where you are now. If your best thinking could have helped you out of this situation, it would have already happened. In this session, Dr. Porter will help you reframe the past, foster a positive mind-set, and mold the present into a healthy agent for change.

FA08 Trying New Things for a New Beginning

Tapping into the power of your other-than-conscious mind goes beyond doing what you have always done. To be liberated from the defeatist attitude of the past, you must embrace change and try new things. It has been said that if you are a craftsman with only a hammer, you will think everything is a nail. The key to lasting change is in having options. There is nothing wrong with persistence, but those who have created a life free from addiction have done so by developing new ways of thinking and acting. In this session, Dr. Patrick Porter will guide you through the resource organizer where you will discover skills you didn't even know you had.

FA09 Social Housecleaning from the Inside Out

During this session you will visualize cleaning up all the bruised relationships and the pockets of guilt, pain, fear, resentment, and sadness that are stored inside, stuck to shameful past deeds. Dr. Porter will help you through this mental healing by guiding you to that power greater than yourself where you will release the past hurts that may be stopping you from loving other people and yourself. You will learn to trust in the guidance of your higher power right now, in the present.

FA10 Becoming a Bridge-Builder for More Positive Relationships

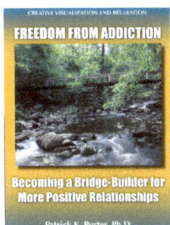

Being a bridge-builder means that cleaning up your past becomes a way of life. As you enter this working relationship with your other-than-conscious mind, Dr. Porter will guide you through your next step, which is to grow in understanding and effectiveness. This is no overnight matter; it will continue for the rest of your life, one day at a time. With this realization you will learn to be vigilant over the part of you that wants to hold on to selfishness, dishonesty, resentment, and fear. When these crop up, you will trust the power greater than yourself to remove them.

FA11 Let Go and Go with the Flow (safe place)

In this process, you will create an internal compass to help you stay the course free from addiction. Dr. Porter will teach you techniques to keep you grounded in reality so that the old attitudes, behaviors, or beliefs that brought out the addictive behaviors stay at bay while new more appropriate behaviors are formed. You will learn to keep your options in a safe place by keeping conscious contact with that power that is greater than you.

FA12 Taking Care of Today by Planning a Bright Future

Dr. Porter will help you stay focused on the most important moment in time, NOW. By taking care of today and staying with a one-day-at-a-time philosophy, you can look forward to a bright and compelling future. This visualization will open you to unlimited possibilities as you make your mind available as a tool for sharing your recovery success on a daily basis.

FA13 Staying Connected to Your Higher Power

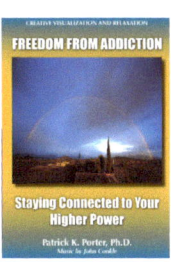

The real secret to remaining free from addiction for a lifetime involves a spiritual awakening. When Dr. Porter did his research, he found that those who stayed connected to this infinite stream of intelligence stayed free from the addictions of the past and kept a fresh perspective on today. Problem solving takes on a new level of creativity when you are connected to this power greater than yourself. You will learn a simple technique that is already being used by thousands to stay connected. You will also be amazed by how simple it is when you trust in the process of change.

Mental Coaching For Golf
Patrick K. Porter, Ph.D.

Efficient golfers know how to relax and let their minds take over. Now, thanks to these creative visualization and relaxation (CVR) processes, you'll learn to see yourself as a calm, confident golfer. You deserve to take pleasure in your time on the course. Thanks to CVR, you'll finally be able to let go of frustration and focus on every stroke—meaning you'll not only play better, but you'll also enjoy the game more than ever!

GF01 - Optimize the Risk Zone for Golf

You've never experienced a practice session like this one! Follow along with Dr. Patrick Porter as he guides you onto the driving range in your mind. Once there, you'll practice each swing, letting go of negative thoughts and allowing the clubs to do what they were designed to do—send the ball straight to the target. From now on, you'll address each ball knowing with certainty that you can see the perfect shot in your mind and achieve it in your actions.

GF02 - Develop the Attitude of a Champion

Champions understand that good outcomes come from good shots. With this dynamic process, you'll find it easy to think positive thoughts and accept each shot as it comes. You'll no longer spend time feeling distracted, over-analyzing your game, blaming the conditions of the course, or getting angry over a bad lie. Instead, you'll admire the trajectory of a well-struck drive, a clean chip shot, or a perfectly sunk putt, as you play and think like a champion!

GF03 - Concentration: Your Key To Consistency

Most golf professionals consider concentration to be the key to playing golf… but almost no one teaches it. In this energizing process by Dr. Patrick Porter, he'll teach you to achieve the concentration you need simply by sitting back, relaxing, and letting go of all stress and confusion. You'll learn to block out distractions, focus like never before, and discover the concentration that will help you play the best golf of your life!

GF04 - Discover the Confidence of a Tiger

Even golfing greats get nervous when their game is on the line. Now you can sit back and relax with this revitalizing session while you learn to face any part of the course with complete self-assurance. You have good instincts—you just have to trust them! From now on, you will, as you awaken ready to use the positive power of your mind… while your golfing buddies marvel at your newfound confidence.

GF05 - Tame Your Tempo and Score

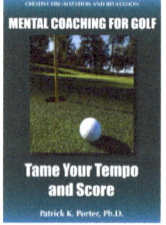

Because the average swing lasts less than two seconds, there's no time to make corrections on the course. That's why it's important to maintain a tempo during your game. Now you can sit back, relax, and let this refreshing session instill the skills you need to look at your game from the outside in, set your perfect tempo, lower your score and, most importantly, enjoy your game to the fullest.

GF06 - Rehearse Excellence and Eliminate Execution Errors

On the golf course your imagination can be your most powerful ally or your worst enemy. With this invigorating session by Dr. Patrick Porter, you'll learn to visualize the ideal shot each and every time you address the ball. Once you imagine the feeling of accomplishment you get from making all the right choices at the tee, you'll be able to stand back and enjoy your perfectly executed drive!

GF07 - Release Pressure and Tension

Tension is normal under certain circumstances—such as during a match—but it can also ruin your game. Thanks to this stimulating session, you'll be able to release pressure and tension under any circumstances. Loosen up, take a deep breath, and let the pressure roll away as you experience your ultimate relaxation both on and off the course.

GF08 Gain Finesse and Lower Your Score

When you step up to the tee box expecting to win, you unleash the power of your mind to plan and produce the perfect round of golf. Research shows the mind doesn't know the difference between real and imagined. Dr. Patrick Porter will teach you techniques that will prove to you how five minutes of visualization can be equal to two hours of physical practice! With this mental edge you will have more fun on the course than ever before.

GF09 Golf is a Mind Game... Play It!

Have you ever wondered what's in the mind of the world's greatest golfers? With this powerful modeling technique, you will be imagining what it's like to take a ride inside the mind of the golfers you most admire. Can you imagine the strokes you will shave off your score as you take advantage of his or her years of golf mastery? With this visualization you will be guided into the realm of infinite possibility where you can master each and every phase of the game you love.

GF10 Master the Course, Master Your Round

Hitting the longest drive or sinking the unsinkable putt might be fun, but it doesn't always equal victories or low scores. Golf is a mind game you play against yourself. By learning how to play within yourself, knowing your strengths and weaknesses, you will learn to master the game. Now you can immediately improve your handicap by playing smarter and staying in control... even in the most challenging situations.

GF11 Erase Nervousness and Perform Under Pressure

Dr. Patrick Porter will show you how a positive mental attitude will help to reduce nervousness and naturally reduce your score. Relaxation tips will help you release any anger or frustration before you address the ball. This unique visualization process will help you to regain your poise and concentration and, most importantly, control your game. Performing on the big, green stage is a breeze when you harness the power of your mind!

GF12 Three Easy Steps to Great Golf in Any Situation

Putting together a great game is all about routine. In this insightful visualization Dr. Patrick Porter takes you from a good stance to a polished mental attitude and beyond. You'll use these keys to lower your score and enjoy it more as you open your mind to the possibilities. Consistency is key to low scores, and you'll be amazed at how easy and natural it is as you relax and rehearse the fundamentals.

GF13 Golfing in Dream Time... Your Key to the Ultimate Swing

Imagine using the techniques of great inventors like Edison, Einstein and Michelangelo. That's exactly what you will be doing when Dr. Patrick Porter guides you through this powerful and fun visualization. It's been said that what the mind can conceive and believe the body will achieve. This visualization is your personal guide—from hopes and wishes to power and believability. It all starts with mentally rehearsing your goals so the unseen forces of the mind will bring them into reality!

Mental Coaching for hCG Phase I & II Success

Human Chorionic Gonadotropin (hCG) has been used for weight loss since 1954 when Dr. Albert T. Simeon, a British-physician, found that hCG injections allowed dieters to manage easily on 500 calories per day. You can learn more about this diet by reading his book, Pounds and Inches.

Dr. Simeon found that hCG could suppress appetite, burn stored fat, as well as redistribute fat from the hips, thighs and waist. While the treatment works well on its own, Dr. Porter's Creative Visualization and Relaxation (CVR) support program can make following the diet protocol easier than ever.

The series will work with hCG in the injection, sublingual, homeopathic or pill form. It is designed to reduce stress and enhance motivation during Phase II of Dr. Simeon's protocol, which is while actually taking hCG and eating the very low calorie diet.

Note: You should never use hCG without the help of a licensed health care professional.

Phase I

HCG-Phase1-01 Detox for Fat Burning Support

Setting up your body for success by detoxifying is not only a good idea, but a necessity, as your liver needs to be ready to flush out the toxins while the HCG eliminates the dark fat in the body. With this session, Dr. Porter will help you kick-start your cleanse program by preparing you for rapid fat loss. With every breath and every move you are creating waste products in your body. Seasonal cleansing helps remove the Western Lifestyle toxins from your body. With this CVR session you will discover the positive benefits of an internal cleanse.

HCG-Phase1-02- Detoxifying the Mind

Research shows that all of us have surprisingly high concentrations of toxins in our blood due to air pollution. This session is designed to keep you focused on staying on the cleanse program and also ridding your mind of the negative thoughts that build up in your daily life from work, family and friends. No matter how "great" your every day diet is, you'll never be able to combat toxins that enter your body daily without the help of herbs. Many toxins are fat-soluble - they are stored in our fat cells for months and slowly released over time. This release becomes intensified by the rapid fat loss from using HCG. So while your body and mind are purging you of toxins, Dr. Porter will help you stay focused on the health of your body for optimum success.

HCG-Phase1-03 Reinforcing the Cleanse

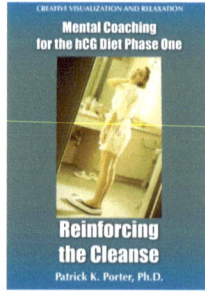

Your liver is supposed to burn fat – if it is overworked from too many other things like cholesterol, environmental toxins or pesticides, when does it have time to burn fat? It doesn't! So your body stores that too. This is why during this session Dr. Porter will help you to remain motivated to follow through and stay on the cleanse program so your liver is in the best possible place to metabolize the fat from Phase II of your program. Doing this right is key to getting the lasting results you want for your body!

Phase II

HCGPhase2-01 – Staying Focused on hCG

The biggest problem with most diets is that losing weight in a healthy way is slow and painful. hCG eliminates this issue. Dieters on Phase II generally lose 1-2 pounds a day without physical hunger. However, the diet is strict and it only works if you stick to the protocol. Dr. Porter created this session to eliminate the old dieter's mindset that craves immediate gratification. In its place you will develop an iron will to stick to the plan for maximum weight loss success.

HCG-Phase2-02 – Water – Your Key to hCG Success

Dr. Simeon states in his book that the dieter should drink about 2 liters or more of water per day. Many people are afraid that drinking so much will make them retain more water. This is an incorrect notion as the body is more inclined to store water when intake falls below its normal requirements. This process will help you easily consume the ideal amount of water so that the mobilized fat can safely exit the body. Not only that, you'll be building this healthy behavior for the rest of your life.

HCG-Phase2-03 – Planning Your Protein

To get the same great results with hCG that so many others have, there requires a degree of planning. It's recommended that you consume 3 ½ ounces of lean protein twice a day. With this session, while the hCG is working to reset your hypothalamus, you will create the mental drive to stay on track. This powerful combination will help you develop both the mind and body of a naturally thin person.

HCG-Phase2-04 – Unlock Your Body's Natural Energy

Balancing out your vegetables and fruit on the hCG diet is key to lasting results. Dr. Porter has created this CVR session to help you focus on the benefits of these fresh organic foods and how they serve your body. While the hCG is working to eliminate cravings, this session will help you recognize the abundant energy that comes from eating live foods.

HCG-Phase2-05 – Tracking Results

Research has shown that what is not measured is not achieved. For lasting results, the habit of monitoring not only the foods you consume but your body's weight will put you back in control while on the diet and, most importantly, after you have reached your target weight.

HCG-Phase2-06 – Breaking Through Plateaus

Not everyone experiences a plateau, but it is nice to know that on the hCG diet there is a fat busting technique that can quickly have you back to melting off 1-2 pounds a day. While others stress about plateaus, you will learn a technique to put you back on the fast track to weight loss success.

Healing Meditations for Child Abuse Survivors
Inspired by the Reaching Out Child Abuse Monument

This series by Dr. Patrick Porter is inspired by Dr. Michael Irving's Reaching Out Child Abuse Monument. These visualizations will assist you in seeing yourself as a remarkable person who has the courage to live through adversity and rise above and beyond a kind of cruelty that never should have happened. You will see that you have a hopeful, problem-solving spirit with a commitment to make more of your life.

Your survival through adversity was heroic, which means you have all the power and resources you need to create a positive mind and a vibrant and enjoyable life. You will be encouraged to think comforting thoughts and to know the ways in which you are safe. These meditations will help you to recognize that the trauma occurred a long time ago. You now have the comfort of distance and the power to move forward. Listening will help you get grounded as you come to understand that a memory is not abuse; memories are thoughts, and feelings and are within your power to change. You can embrace the power of your inner wisdom. You can release the emotions of the past. You will realize that no matter what has happened, you get better and better everyday, and you will find pleasure and comfort in the world you create. What you imagine is what you become.

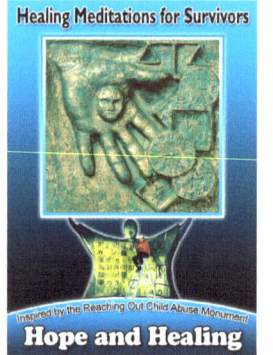

HMS01 – Meditation on Hope and Healing
In this meditation, you will reflect on hope as your birthright and as one of the most powerful forces in the universe. You will let healing hope radiate through your spirit and will focus on thoughts that bring hope, comfort and calm. You will meditate on the people you can lean on for support and turn to for nurturing. You will contemplate thoughts that bring you hope, and that move you closer to comfort and calm. The hopes of your dreams are what you receive.

HMS02 – Meditation for Empowerment
During this meditation, you will reflect on your inner strengths and the empowerment that comes from believing in yourself. You will meditate on feelings associated with your important accomplishments and how others see your strengths. In acknowledging your empowerment and victories, you can come to trust your inner voice and intuition. You will dream big and know you can follow those dreams.

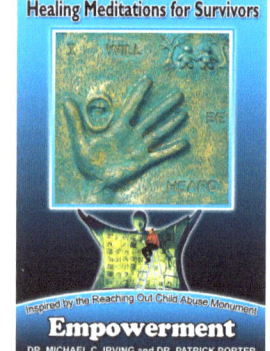

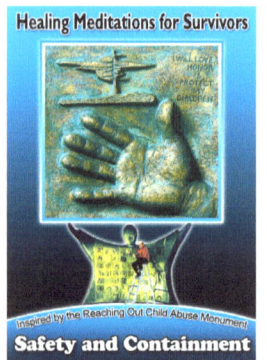

HMS03 – Meditation for Safety and Containment
This mediation will help you create safety and containment through visualizing a safe room. You will explore what you need for your individual safe room and create it as your perfect place of relaxation. You will also practice separation and distancing though a locked box or other container. This meditation is a celebration of the power, resiliency and amazement within your inner wisdom and other-than-conscious mind.

HMS04 – Meditation for Healing Shame
Abuse survivors often carry a heavy burden of shame and humiliation. This meditation will help you free yourself from these destructive and limiting feelings. It will assist you with internalizing the truth that the abuse was not your fault and that the shame does not belong to you. You will feel your power to release stuck patterns and beliefs of the past that no longer serve you. You will release shame and replace the emotion with joy and freedom.

HMS05 – Meditation on Trust
Abuse robs the birthright of trust. Through this meditation, you will reawaken your innate ability to trust. You will explore what you need in your life and environment to feel safe and secure. Experiencing your "antennae" for trust and for mistrust will empower you. Safe, trusting people will fill your thoughts and begin to appear in your life.

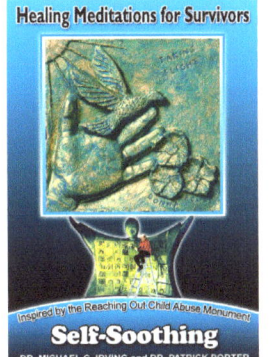

HMS06 – Meditation on Self-Soothing
This meditation will support and nourish the positive and comforting feelings already inside of you so they will grow and blossom. You will practice breathing in calming energy and releasing stress as you become more relaxed and self-aware. Listening to this meditation will help you find more and more ways to self-sooth and nurture yourself.

HMS07 – Meditation for Grief and Letting Go
This meditation will support you in moving through and beyond the grief associated with child abuse. You will acknowledge and accept the presence of grief and then give it permission to be resolved and released. The meditation will provide you the release and freedom that letting go of the past creates. You will then take that freedom with you into your present and future.

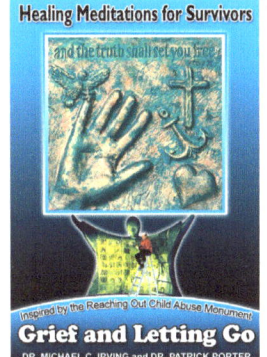

HMS08 Meditation for Healing the Inner Child
This meditation will assist you in connecting with the innocence of your inner child. You will assure your inner child that there is safety and benefit in healing and letting go. You will help your inner child make sense of the hurt from long ago so you can restore your feelings of worthiness and reclaim your ability to love and be loved.

HMS09 – Meditation on Celebrating Victory
This meditation will focus on celebrating the victory of having survived and thrived through the adversities of childhood and the challenging process of healing. You will reflect on the many ways you can be proud of yourself. Just to get through your childhood was an extraordinary achievement. Once you acknowledge this, your ability to embrace life today will be magnificent. You are a hero and your healing from adversity will make a difference in the lives of others.

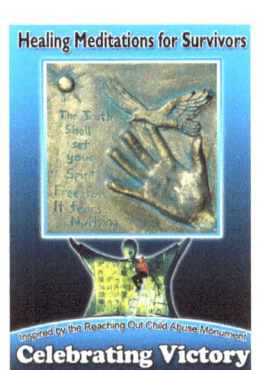

HMS10 – Meditation to Heal Self-Blame
This meditation focuses on helping you to let go of self-blame and the guilt and destructive behaviors that frequently accompany a history of child abuse. You will focus on the reality that you did the best you could against insurmountable odds. This process will help you recognize that there is nothing wrong with you. As you release self-blame you will feel joy and freedom, and see yourself as a new you.

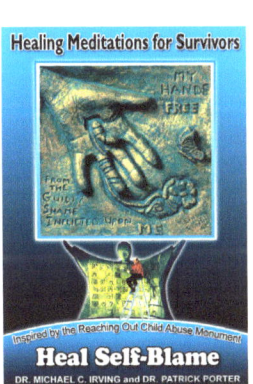

HMS11 – Meditation on Embracing Freedom
Through this meditation you will embrace and celebrate the freedom of having overcome the pain that lasted so long. You will celebrate your freedom and know the past is no longer a chain that binds you. This meditation will assist you with creating an ever-present force of freedom inside of you.

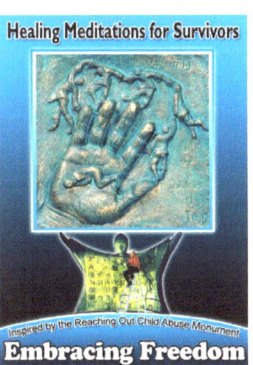

HMS12 – Meditation for Feeling Loved
This meditation focuses on reawakening your basic right to feel loved that was wounded by child abuse. You will reflect on times where you felt loved and notice where the "being loved" feeling is inside of you so you can let that feeling grow. You will meditate on attracting loving people to your life, knowing that what you see is what you create.

HMS13 – Safe Mountain Meadow Retreat
In this meditation you will create a safe mountain meadow retreat as an empowering inner sanctuary you can return to again and again. You will connect with the courage, bravery and life skills you have inside. You will experience your retreat as a protective place of containment and peacefulness. Your mountain meadow retreat will become a safe haven where you can go whenever you need to find refuge from troubling feelings or thoughts.

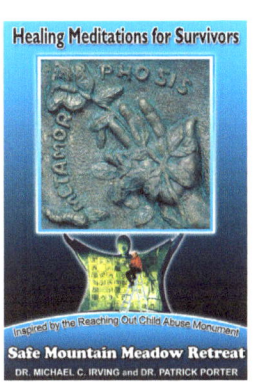

PorterVision's Product Resources

Insomnia Solutions Series

Studies show that insomnia is the most common sleep disorder in the United States. About one-third of the adult population has experienced insomnia at some time and approximately ten percent experience debilitating side effects such as daytime drowsiness, irritability, lack of concentration, and poor memory. When the body doesn't get the deep sleep it needs to recharge and rebuild, the immune system can suffer as well. As frustrating as insomnia may be, there is a solution. In this series, Dr. Patrick Porter (PhD) will help you discover how, by using creative visualization and relaxation (CVR), you can quickly and easily return to a natural sleep cycle and regain your health and vitality.

IS01 – Sleep Deep and Awaken Recharged

When people consider treatment for insomnia, they tend to think first of sleeping pills. But in reality you already possess the most powerful pharmacy on earth—the human mind. Through the power of thought, your brain can release into the bloodstream any number of 30,000 different neuro-chemicals. Today Dr. Porter is going to show you how, by using creative visualization and relaxation (CVR), you can dispel the pressure and frustration associated with insomnia and attain restful sleep. You will discover new ways to focus on your innate ability to fall asleep and allow deep delta sleep—the most restful form of sleep—to come naturally.

IS02 – Planning a Restful Night's Sleep

In this process, Dr. Porter will teach you to look forward to sleep. You will train your mind to think differently by removing all anxiety at the approach of sundown, throughout the evening hours, and at bedtime. During this visualization, you will re-associate with the dreamy, drowsy state of sleepiness you've experienced in the past so that you can master the ability to sleep without the aid of medications. Even if your problem started with anxiety or panic attacks, you will experience the release of both and eliminate negativity from your sleep cycle.

IS03 – Making Peace with Your Body for Deep Restful Sleep

People who have trouble sleeping tend to be the same people who try to control situations, people, and events that are beyond their control. With this CVR session, Dr. Porter will help you put your life into perspective so you can rediscover your natural sleeping patterns. You will release the unconscious need to react with fear, both consciously and unconsciously, about any situation that is not within your control. At the same time, through the relaxation response, you will be making natural physical changes (slowing your heartbeat, lowering your blood pressure, regulating your breathing) to prevent the panic attacks that may otherwise arise during light stages of sleep. You will find yourself drifting peacefully into deep delta sleep and awakening in the morning feeling rested, relaxed, and renewed.

IS04 - Sleep Deep & Let Go of Unwanted Fears Forever

During deep relaxation and sleep, physical changes occur that are a natural part of the process of falling into slumber. Feelings such as floating, being in a trance, or of a slowed heartbeat are common. These are natural parts of the sleep cycle. You will learn to allow these changes to guide you into deep sleep. Dr. Porter will teach a simple visualization and relaxation technique that will lead you into deep delta sleep - the deepest, most rejuvenating kind of sleep there is. These two simple words you will train your brain to fall fast asleep.

IS05 - Going with the Flow Day & Night

In this session, Dr. Porter will help you to eliminate the fears and frustrations that may be keeping you from a good night's rest. You will learn to think differently during the day so you can rid yourself of anxious thoughts and worries. At the same time, new thought patterns will disrupt past conditioning that may be causing you to physically react to stressful situations. Since you will no longer be mentally escalating negative thoughts and emotions during the day, you will be free to sleep comfortably all night long.

Freedom From Irritable Bowel Syndrome

When Dr. Patrick Porter (Ph.D.) was asked by his clients to help with Irritable bowel syndrome (IBS) back in the early 1980's he first thought that relaxation technique could help this problem. Then a client brought in a series of magazine articles showing that in the United Kingdom the first thing a medical doctor would do is refer them to a therapist for creative imagery and relaxation training.

This is when his quest to help his clients with this common problem with the intestines. It is believed that in most cases IBS is more of a thinking problem than a physical problem where a persons intestines squeeze too hard or not hard enough and cause food to move too quickly or too slowly through the intestines. IBS usually begins around age 20 and is more common in women.

IBS01 -- Mental Tips on Controlling Your IBS Symptoms

During this foundation session Dr. Porter teaches you to take the time to reduce their stresses and apprehensions. The key to relief is becoming familiar with the mind/body connection and to learn that you can eliminate the emotional triggers that put you out of control.

IBS02 -- Being Physically & Mentally Balanced

This session helps the listener manage IBS symptoms by letting the users understand the benefits of allowing both mind and body to work together towards the goal of relief. Science has shown that the best way to handle IBS is to eat a healthy diet, avoid foods that seem to make you feel worse and find ways to handle your stress.

IBS03 – Stress Buster Your Key to IBS Relief

With stress being a symptom that may cause the listener to get worse when they travel, attend social events or change your daily routine. Dr. Porter has created a simple technique that puts you instantly back in control. Our bodies are designed with the flight or fight response but with the new science of Creative Visualization and Relaxation (CVR) you can learn the "Relaxation Response." This technique will work whether your symptoms get worse if you don't eat enough healthy foods or after you've eaten a big meal.

IBS04 -- Using Your Mind to Regulate Your Body

You will learn to uses the power of suggestion to enable to visualize the control and speed of peristaltic waves of the GI tract that will lead to a normal bowel movement. Whether you bloating and gas the key is to relaxation and bring the body back into homeostasis. This can be done with proper diet and relaxation.

IBS05 – Staying True to Your Body for IBS Support

Food sensitivity can be a major cause of IBS and during this session Dr. Porter will guide you through mental exercises where you will plan to avoid the foods that cause the problem to worsen. You will also use visualization to creatively increase your fiber. Health science has discovered that fiber can be helpful because it improves how the intestines work. You will relax and plan to use the 2 types of fiber. Soluble fiber helps both diarrhea and constipation.

IBS06 -- Tips on controlling IBS for a Healthy Life

In this self directed session you will learn a breakthrough technique that you can use to eliminate stress and stay focused on healthy living. Dr. Porter will reinforce the elimination of old stress that in the past triggered the old symptoms of IBS. You will build a time-line for change by building a support system including your family doctor or health care provider. Staying mental prepared for success you will continue to discover ways to deal with stress, such as exercise, relaxation training or meditation. This technique will help you if the symptoms get worse when you're under stress, such as when you travel, attend social events or change your daily routine. You will plan to eat a varied healthy diet and avoid foods high in fat. Drink plenty of water.

PorterVision's Product Resources

Life-Mastery Series

Throughout your life, from parents, teachers, and society, you were taught *what* to think. With the breakthrough processes of creative visualization and relaxation, you are going to discover *how* to think. With this knowledge you will literally become a software engineer for your own mind. On the Life-Mastery journey, you will explore the processes that best suit your needs for creating limitless personal improvement and success in your life.

LM01 - Operating in Your Optimal Risk Zone

The startling truth is, all human beings must have risk in their lives to thrive and feel fulfilled. Listen to this session and you'll know how to leverage risk for personal advancement and easily accomplish your loftiest goals. The dot com bust turned risk into a four letter word. Yet executives and companies that don't employ risk can face extinction. In creating the Optimal Risk Zone, Dr. Patrick Porter researched the mindset of the controlled risk-takers who launched the high-tech industry. Then, using CVR, those thoughts and behaviors can be virtually downloaded into your mind.

LM02 - Ask, Believe & Receive Visualization

The universe operates on specific laws. These *invisible* laws are always *manifesting* your physical reality. The universe never *tries* anything; it only *does*. This visualization calls upon the *Law of Attraction*, and helps you to become a conscious creator. You will discover how you designed, at the core of your being, to be an active participant in the enfoldment of your relationships, wealth and happiness. Now, without even trying or having to struggle, success will come as naturally as the sun rises and sets. Imagine how much easier your life can become when you are in perfect harmony with universal law!

LM03 - The Secret Power of Self-talk

On average, you give yourself over 5,000 messages a day. With this process you will discover how to weed your mental garden of negative thoughts and to sow new, more positive thoughts. You will use the same four-step process that has helped thousands of people neutralize fear, anxiety and worry. Using CVR, you discover the secret power of self-talk to easily create the habits, patterns, and beliefs that can put your success on autopilot.

LM04 – Activate the Magnetic Power of Your Dreams

Many of the great inventors of the past discovered that your dreams are a powerful way to communicate with your other-than-conscious mind. You will unlock the most powerful computer on earth as you discover creative ways to use your dreams to visualize solutions to everyday problems. Get ready to step out of the past and into a bright and compelling future!

LM05 – Become A Personal Success Magnet

With this CVR process, Dr. Patrick Porter will guide you through powerful and easy techniques for attracting success into your life. Your new thoughts will act as a magnet that draws the right people and opportunities to you, and guides you in making the right decisions. Sit back and relax in the laboratory of your mind as you tap into your other-than-conscious storehouse of success-breeding thoughts—the thoughts that will draw success to you as naturally as you draw your next breath.

LM06 – Whole Brain Motivation & Unending Drive

During this CVR journey, you will discover new ways of tapping into the creative right side of your brain. Then, using the left logical side of the brain, you will create a timeline for success. When you harness the power of whole brain thinking, you can accomplish even the most difficult tasks with ease. The balanced success that others only dream of will be yours as you master this visualization.

PorterVision Product Catalog

LM07 – Step On The Fast Track To Personal Success

Sir Isaac Newton once said that if he had achieved anything with his work, such as his laws of motion and gravity, it was "by standing on the shoulders of giants." With this process, you will explore what I call *The Picasso Factor* and find out why it was easy for Gandhi, Einstein and other masters to put their success on autopilot. By using the principle of mentoring found in this visualization, you will tap into your own inner genius and be on the fast track to success. What is *The Picasso Factor*? You'll have to listen to find out!

LM08 – Enthusiasm, Focus & Flexibility… Your Keys To Success

Imagine the improvements you can make in your life once you activate the powerful storehouse of your other-than-conscious mind that will give you all the enthusiasm, focus and flexibility you need on a day-to-day basis. During this visualization, Dr. Patrick Porter will guide you to find your own internal success coach, who will take you step-by-step in the direction of your goals. With this mental exercise you will easily manifest your dreams into reality.

LM09 – Harness The Power Of Change

You will discover why *change*, the only constant in the universe, can be your most powerful ally. When you let go of the fear of change, and harness its power instead, you are tapping into the most potent force in the universe. When you try new things in the laboratory of your mind, you erase fear and embrace the action steps necessary to maximize your results.

LM10 – Awaken Your Senses and Create Your Future

Your senses can be likened to the keyboard on a computer. Through sight, sound, touch, smell and taste, your brain takes in information from the world around you. Now you can learn to use your senses to magnetize success into your life. It becomes simple to be the person you were destined to be when you create change at the other-than-conscious level of your mind. It's literally as easy as seeing, hearing, feeling and maybe even tasting or smelling the future of your dreams.

LM11 – Power Phrases For Powerful Actions

Discover how affirmative words and phrases can create a powerful mental image of a healthy, wealthy and vibrant new you. You will notice how these positive affirmations let your other-than-conscious mind quickly put into motion all the right actions at the right time to lead you to a life filled with the results you really want

.

LM12 – Eliminate Negative Thinking and Harness The Power of Optimism

You can't help but be bombarded with negative thoughts and beliefs; it's on the radio, television and in the newspaper. With this powerful process, Dr. Patrick Porter will guide you into altered states, where you'll discover ways of breaking through to your creative optimistic mind. Once there you will be visualizing solutions to your life challenges. Imagine what you will create in your life as you eliminate the negative and let the flow of optimistic thinking create instantaneous solutions.

LM13 - Transform Procrastination into Total Motivation

All behaviors are useful in the right context. During this CVR process, Dr. Porter will guide you through a seven-step transformation process that will end procrastination and convert that energy into the usable motivation you'll need to complete tasks, start new projects, or live the healthy lifestyle you always dreamed of. Using the power of possibility has never been easier as you relax and realize your goals.

LM14 – Journey to the Creativity Zone

In today's stress-filled, hectic world it is often difficult to quiet your mind enough to tap your innate creativity. Yet for many of us, creativity is essential to our work performance. And, for all of us, it is vital for leading a balanced life. As you kick back and relax, Dr. Porter guides to a mind state where you can enhance any creative endeavor. This session is truly an inner journey to the place in your mind where ideas abound and solutions are readily available.

Medical Series
Patrick K. Porter, Ph.D.

MS001 – De-Stress and Lower Blood Pressure

The physiological benefits of deep relaxation and visualization are well documented. During this creative visualization process you will learn to achieve the relaxation response—a state known to unlock your brain's potential for de-stressing your body and returning your blood pressure to a healthy level. Known benefits of the relaxation response also include a lower respiratory rate, a slower pulse, relaxed muscles, and an increase in alpha brain wave activity—everything that makes for a healthier you!

MS02 – Pre-Surgery Calm for Better Healing

For years physicians and therapist have used guided relaxation, intense concentration, and focused attention to achieve deep relaxation and heightened states of awareness prior to surgery. Now, through the science of creative visualization and relaxation (CVR), you can easily benefit from these powerful processes. Patients using these techniques are known to have less pain, require less pain medication, and enjoy a more rapid recovery.

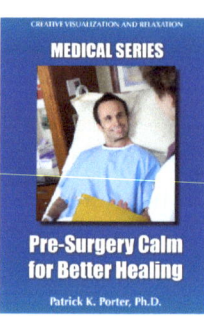

MS03 – Post-Surgery Stress Relief for a Healthy Mind and Body

CVR is a relaxation technique that uses concentration and deep breathing to calm the mind and put your body in the best possible state for repair and healing. What could be easier than to sit back, relax, and let the stress of surgery and recovery melt away?

MS04 – Soothing Pain Relief for Rapid Healing

With CVR you are learning to use imagery—engaging your imagination—to create sights, sounds, smells, tastes, and other sensations that create the relaxation response, a state known to trigger your body into producing its own natural analgesia. With this technique Dr. Patrick Porter will teach you how psychological changes create physical effects, and vice versa—a skill you can use for the rest of your life!

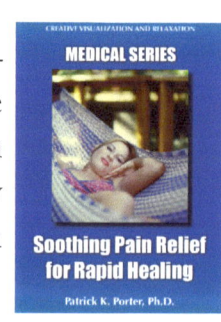

MS05 – Rid Your Mind of Pre-Surgery Jitters

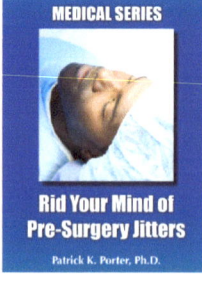

CVR can help ease fears and soothe anxiety before surgery. With this process you are guided into a positive resource state where you rid your body and mind of the jitters, worries, and uncertainties that can be a part of surgery or medical procedures.

MS06 – Mentally Prepare for Your Procedure

Dr. Porter will train you to focus your attention on the one thing that matters as you go into surgery—relaxing. Through this creative process you will become so focused on the success of the procedure that you will easily ignore anything else going on around you. The result? Relief from anxiety and the development of a positive mental attitude.

MS07 – Relax and Heal After Surgery

Relaxing after surgery is a key to healing. With this CVR process, you can do quick little mental healing sessions throughout the day. Why focus on stress or pain when you can do your body so much good by concentrating on the healing process? It's easier than you think!

MS08 – Mental Relaxation During a Procedure

In some cases it makes sense to use CVR during a minor surgery. With your doctor's approval, you can use this session throughout the procedure to help you relax and focus on positive images. For many people this kind of mental relaxation not only helps decrease stress, but can actually reduce or eliminate the discomfort associated with medical procedures.

MS09 – Staying Relaxed After Your Procedure

Meditation has proven to help patients with post-surgery sleep disturbances, disorders associated with tension, and chronic pain. Like meditation, CVR promotes wellness. With this process you learn creative ways to relax your mind and body so you sleep deeply, rest completely, and are less impacted by tension and pain. The result? An easier, more rapid recovery and often less need for pain medication.

MS10 – Post-Surgery Visualization for Body Mending

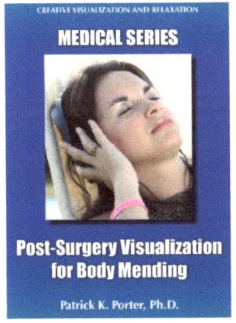

When you have less anxiety before a procedure, you will experience less pain later. With this simple-to-use technique you will discover ways to picture your body mending after surgery. You can use also it to eliminate insomnia so you will sleep deeply, which is an important priority since most healing takes place during sleep.

Mind-Over-Menopause
Patrick K. Porter, Ph.D.

For many women mid-life can be a time of uncertainty and loss. For some the loss of fertility and the perceived loss of youth can cause depression and anxiety. At the same time, the body's response to the decrease in hormones can create any number of symptoms—hot flashes, night sweats, weight gain, itchy skin, mood swings, lost libido, headaches, and irregular cycles are just of few of the menopausal challenges women face. In the midst of all these changes, relationships can suffer as loved ones start to ask, "What happened to the caring, loving woman we once knew?" Now you can reclaim that woman, along with all the strength, confidence, and wisdom you gained in the first half of your life. This series takes you way beyond mind over matter—it's mind over menopause!

MM01 - Balance Your Mood, Balance Your Life

With this session you will use creative visualization and relaxation to help balance your mood, harness positive mental energy, and use your innate creative power to produce much-needed balance in your life during this time of change and uncertainty. You will stop focusing on what you've lost, and discover all that you've gained!

MM02 - Creating Harmony With the Cycles of Life

Using your mind you will activate the powerful calming effects produced by your own brain chemistry. When you relax and let your mind experience a cascade of positive thoughts and images, you will find that the emotional ups and downs of menopause become a distant memory.

MM03 - Mental Skills to Help You Master Menopause

With this creative visualization and relaxation process, you will be given time to plan your life from a new perspective. You will learn to view menopause as a rite of passage—one that gives you confidence and inner worth. !

MM04 - Relax and Control Night Sweats and Hot Flashes

Now you can greatly reduce or eliminate the hot flashes and night sweats typically associated with menopause. Relaxation therapy is a natural remedy for hot flashes and many women have found lasting relief with this method. Now, with the added dimension of creative visualization, you will discover that you can master the cooling effects of your mind, and you will feel your body naturally cooling off as well!

MM05 - Eliminate "Brain Fog" and Sharpen Your Memory

Has menopause got you in a fog? Do you sometimes wonder where your memory went? During menopause many women describe this lack of focus and concentration as "brain fog." When the fog sets in, sometimes even the easiest tasks can seem confusing or overwhelming.

MM06 - Coping With Emotional Changes During Menopause

Get ready to see yourself as the woman you've chosen to be! In this session, you will be building healthy coping mechanisms for conquering mood swings, overcoming anxiety, and regaining your libido. Thanks to a little-known side benefit to deep relaxation, you will also notice improved concentration, soaring energy levels, and freedom from the irritability of the past.

MM07 - Get Connected in Times of Uncertainty

Many menopausal women describe feeling disconnected from their bodies, as if they are suddenly uncomfortable within their own skins. Using your innate creativity, you will learn new tools to rid your mind of these confusing, and often unpleasant, thoughts and feelings. You will discover a new sense of connectedness and purpose, and your "woman's intuition" will be back in full swing!

MM08 - Eliminate Fatigue and Boost Your Energy

Tap into the flow that is your personal power and feel your fatigue and low energy levels melt away. While relaxing with this process you will learn to own your own personal space and will develop an emotional drive to make your wellbeing a top priority.

MM09 - Mastering the Physical Changes of Menopause

When you tap into the power of possibility thinking and engage the internal pharmacy within your brain, you can eliminate gastrointestinal distress and nausea or those dreadful headaches. During this session you will put a plan into action for controlling weight gain, bloating, or that tingling or itchy skin so many women experience.

MM10 - Tips for Quick Menopausal Relief

Sometimes you need relief right now! This session is your answer. You can just sit back, relax and let these tips for reducing stress, clearing your head, and regrouping take you away. Within the session you will create a new, healthier lifestyle that includes cutting back on caffeine, alcohol, and spicy foods the easy way.

MM11 - Making Peace With Your Body

This session is like Tai Chi for the mind. Discover new ways to handle those unusual menopausal symptoms such as that annoying buzzing in your head, electric shock sensations, dry mouth, dry eyes, dizziness, or lightheadedness. When you learn to practice mental Tai Chi, the transition through mid-life and menopause can be far easier than you think!

MM12 - Pain Control and Menopause

When you have sore joints and muscles, cramps or headaches, you can use this simple yet powerful process to put your pain at bay so you can enjoy your everyday activities. Of course, pain is a signal from the body and any undiagnosed pain should be reported to your medical professional.

MM13 - Three Easy Steps To Regaining Balance

Many women experience irregular cycles and mood swings while transitioning into menopause. Some women may even experience sudden heart palpitations, intense anxiety or feelings of panic. Now you can find your way back to center quickly and easily. These steps, once mastered, can work for you even in the most difficult situations. With this session you will learn the three simple steps needed to regain balance in your life no matter the circumstances.

Pain-Free Lifestyle Program
Patrick K. Porter, Ph.D.

Persistent pain can have a costly impact on your life. It can lead to depression, loss of appetite, irritability, anger, loss of sleep, withdrawal from social interaction, and an inability to cope. Fortunately, with creative visualization and relaxation (CVR), pain can almost always be controlled. (CVR) helps you eliminate pain while you relax, revitalize, and rejuvenate. You deserve to be free of your pain—and now you can be, thanks to CVR!

PF01 - Tapping into a Pain-Free Lifestyle

Dr. Patrick Porter will guide you through a simple exercise to transform pain into relaxation. You'll tap into your body's innate ability to heal itself, allowing the healing process to happen while you take a relaxing mental vacation. Pain will lose all power over you as you learn to relax away your pain and enjoy your life free from discomfort.

PF02 - Activate Your Mental Pharmacy

In this dynamic process, you'll unlock your body's natural pharmacy, flushing pain from your body and neutralizing all discomfort. You will so galvanize your mind's healing capacity, all you'll have to do is say the word to release pain, fear and anxiety. Most importantly, you'll have this healing power at your fingertips—when and where you need it most.

PF03 - Starting the Day Pain-Free

In this motivational session, Dr. Patrick Porter will show you that living pain-free is as simple as saying, "So-Hum." Which means, transporting yourself to a pain-free state can be as easy as breathing! You'll be able to bury your pain in the past and awaken each morning pain-free.

PF04 - Developing A Pain-free Future

Dr. Patrick Porter will train you to relax deeply with this process that helps you break through the pain barrier. Discover creative ways to unleash the power of your mind to create your future where you are living a pain-free lifestyle. Learn to go to sleep with certainty that you have the skills to awaken each and every day free from discomfort.

PF05 - Removing Discomfort and Pain

With this creative visualization, Dr. Patrick Porter will help you learn how positive imaging can be your key to a lifetime of relief from unwanted pain or discomfort. Let these relaxing suggestions melt your pain away as you imagine yourself in a state of optimum health and harmony for you.

PF06 - Train the Brain to Create Instant Anesthesia

Dr. Patrick Porter will train you to take these simple steps to link your body and mind so that a free flow of natural analgesia will occur even while you are awake, alert and conscious. You can use this system post-surgery, in the dental chair, or daily to remove arthritis or joint pain. Life gets exciting when you are back in control.

PF07 - You Can Live Naturally Pain Free

With this CVR process, Dr. Patrick Porter provides a thorough summary of the advice and information on how to live naturally pain free, including breathing, visualization and other relaxation techniques. Even if you are using medication, you can use the power of your mind to lessen your discomfort. You may even find that you can lessen or eliminate your need for pain medicine. *Note: Never make changes to your medication without first consulting with your doctor.*

PF08 - Erase Chronic Pain and Enjoy Life Again

Dr. Patrick Porter uses a very compassionate, encouraging visualization process that engages kindness towards yourself and your body. He guides you to a place where you can slowly and gently make peace with your pain. The emphasis throughout this CVR process is on letting acceptance happen, rather than trying to make it happen with your conscious mind and his caring words and soothing voice help guide you through the process.

PF09 - Break the Emotional Bond to Physical Pain

Dr. Patrick Porter uses an advanced time-line technique to help you flex your mind's pain-reducing muscles. You will discover your own power to reduce or eliminate pain by releasing the emotional bonds you may have with your pain. Your focus will be on creating powerful, positive experiences that will, in turn, create the remarkable brain chemicals that work with your body to eliminate discomfort.

PF10 - Develop a Healthy Pain-free Attitude

During this CVR process, you will become aware of any resistance your body may have to becoming pain free. Even though on a conscious level you can't think of a reason for the pain, pain is a signal to the body. The pain could be physical, emotional, mental, or all three. Dr. Patrick Porter will guide you through a discovery of the faculties of your mind that release negativity and move you forward with a life-changing positive attitude about your body and mind.

PF11 - Mend Your Mind, Mend Your Body

With this relaxing process, you will use proven techniques for improving your self-esteem and assertiveness, helping you to feel better about yourself and plan your life more successfully. Dr. Patrick Porter will help you to develop a meaningful relationship between your mind and body, giving you the skills needed for a lifelong pain-free style of living.

PF12 - Develop Instant Pain Relief Triggers

It's easy to develop effective life skills when you have an arsenal of relaxation techniques and pain relief triggers. During this process, Dr. Patrick Porter will teach you useful tools for not only mastering the pain-free state, but for embracing a healthier lifestyle as well. These techniques are valuable in helping you to relieve physical discomfort regardless of whether or not you are currently in pain.

PF13 - Generate the Relaxation Response to Remove Pain

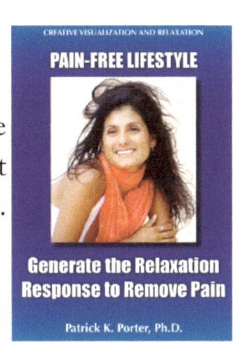

As Dr. Patrick Porter guides you to relax each part of your body, you learn to associate pain-free states in a totally new way. As you relax, you will imagine a healing sanctuary that supports relaxation and your mind's belief in your right to be healthy, strong and vibrant. In this space you feel safe and protected as you visualize healing energy filling your body.

Finding Love and Building Winning Relationships
Patrick K. Porter, Ph.D.
& Michael Irving, Ph.D.

Winning at dating involves building relationship skills that you can apply to the world of dating and romance. With Dr. Michael Irving's powerful techniques, and Dr. Patrick Porter's guiding voice, this program provides you a step-by-step plan for creating a winning attitude and positive outlook, the key life skills needed to succeed at dating and in romantic relationships. Dr. Porter & Dr. Irving understand that finding a date is never easy, but you can increase your odds dramatically by harnessing the right attitude, developing the habit of positive self-talk, and changing any negative beliefs you have created around dating. This program is designed to assist you in developing the positive attitude and success-driven belief system that can make you a winner at dating and relationships.

WR00 – 10-Minute Preview Session: Building Winning Relationships

Relax with this introductory session to awaken your other-than-conscious mind to the myriad of dating possibilities before you. This session is designed to help you awaken the self-confidence within you so you can start feeling comfortable and secure in responding to the dating opportunities presented to you.

WR01 Taking Charge of Your Dating Success

In this session, you will see how the dating game is at your door just waiting for you to embrace it. You will see yourself walking through that door with joy in your heart and a spring in your step. As you take charge of your personal approach to dating, you will find yourself trying new things to look and feel better. Taking more interest in your clothing, hair, and grooming will become second nature to you. Whether your interest in dating is about building a relationship or just having fun, you will rehearse presenting your desires honestly and openly. From that deep inner place in your mind, you develop a natural ability to socialize comfortably. Spending time with like-minded people will become natural to you.

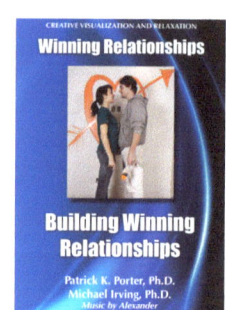

WR02 Overcoming Shyness

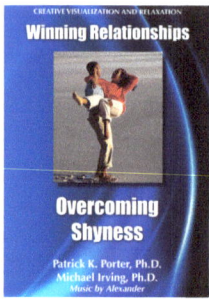

We all have some form of shyness inside that's driven by the fear of rejection. This session will help you eliminate the shyness that inhibits or even paralyzes you from taking up new relationships. The inspiring words in this session will serve to transform your shyness into the confidence that you deserve to radiate. You will create a new you with radiant self-confidence. Your self-assured smile, your interest, your openness, and the confidence you exude will work together in helping you strike up conversations and hold the attention of others.

WR03 Freedom From Criticism ... It's In Your Power

It may seem as if you have spent your entire life trying to make others happy, but this is not how you started your life journey. As a toddler you were okay with just being you; you were a gift to life in every way that is you. Later, when others treated you with negativity, you learned to protect yourself. But the truth is, people were really trying to make up for their own feelings of low self-worth and of not being good enough. You no longer have to internalize other people's insecurities or not-good-enough belief systems. During this session, you will acquire resiliency and learn to rise above criticism at work, home, or in the activities you undertake. Your other-than-conscious mind knows you are perfectly fine just as you are. When you know you are good enough for yourself, you are naturally good enough for others.

WR04 Increase Your Attraction Through Confident Flirting

The art of flirting is a two way dance. The confidence you display is the strongest factor how your flirting is received. After listening to this process, you will feel confident knowing that successful flirting is a natural response. You will see yourself having fun flirting as you comfortably send signals that you are interested and available. You will see yourself smiling, touching, and being playful as you give another person your full attention. In the two-way dance of flirting, you will learn to trust your intuition and other-than-conscious mind to know when the signs of flirting are coming your way. In fact, you will visualize yourself at a dance with a friend who is going to practice the art of flirting with you, allowing you to notice body language and the subtle nuances of flirting.

WR05 Letting Go of Fear and Visualizing Dating Success

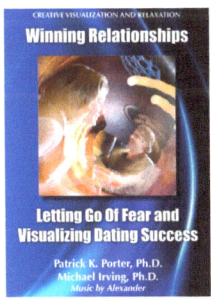

In this session, you are going to visalize a successful date as the new you who enjoys simple, casual, carefree, and fun experiences. You will visualize yourself fully prepared to go on a date with someone you like and who likes you. All hints of nervousness or anxiety have been put to rest. The smile in your eyes says you are glad to be there and you appreciate the person with whom you are sharing the moment. With both your conscious and other-than-conscious mind, you are going to feel and experience a date that turns out the way that you want. Through repeated use of this session, you will notice how each day your confidence and positive expectations of dating get better and the actions you take to improve your world become easier and more natural.

WR06 Finding a Date In The Expansive World Around You

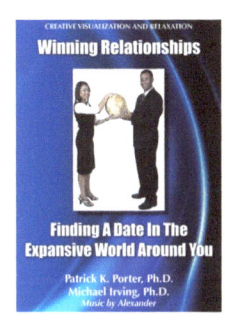

With this session you will learn to integrate looking for dates into your everyday social routine. During this visualization, you discover that you do not need to be pushy, obsessive or aggressive, but you also know that there are opportunities just waiting to present a special someone in your life. You will learn the art of optimism. Connecting with people suitable for dating has never been easier. You find your positive attitude is making it easier every day. You never know when an exciting and adventurous door will open for you. Any negative beliefs about dating will drift away and be replaced with a carefree, positive and confident attitude.

PorterVision's Product Resources

Sales Mastery Series
Patrick K. Porter, Ph.D.

Discover the powerful selling methods of sales masters! When you use this amazing series, you'll build your self-confidence, master your time, and learn to overcome all objections. Visualize and realize your brighter sales future today.

SM01 - Sales Confidence through Self-Confidence
To have confidence in your sales skills, you need confidence in yourself. In this dynamic session, Dr. Patrick Porter will show you how to generate resources you never knew you had. Take control of your own self-confidence in order to organize your thoughts, put priorities in place and take control of your sales… and your life!

SM01 - Supercharge Your Sales Skills
You already have all the abilities you need to become a sales superstar. This exciting process will help you organize those resources to eliminate cold-call reluctance and discover the secrets known by true sales pros. Sit back, relax, and find out how to supercharge your sales skills!

SM03 - Enjoying the Prospecting Game
All sales masters know networking is the key to finding a need and helping prospects fill it. This refreshing process by Dr. Patrick Porter teaches you to develop your infinite referral system and make all the money you desire. When you approach sales with the mindset of a child, prospecting is not only easy… it's fun!

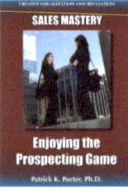

SM04 - Creating Your Sales Success Plan
Use this enjoyable and effortless process to discover quick, easy steps for implementing and working your personal success plan. When you have a plan, you create unlimited success in your sales career, as well as a balanced life at home. It's fun to master your career and your life!

SM05 - The Bigger the Goal, the Better the Result
Sit back and relax as Dr. Patrick Porter shows you how to eliminate small thinking from your sales and your life. Break the chains of old, conscious thought and use your creative mind to create bigger goals and better results. Expand your ability to be flexible around the most difficult people and use quick techniques for closing the sale with even the most negative person.

SM06 - Build Your Personal Success Strategy
Creating balance in your life is easy when you use your other-than-conscious. With this revitalizing process, you'll quickly wipe out procrastination and energize your daily sales activities. Discover your dynamic self-image that's been waiting to shine. When you activate your creative genius, your possibilities are endless!

SM07 - Rehearse Using Questions to Understand Your Prospect's Business
Enter the theater of your mind, where you visualize and realize your sales goals! Discover the ease of working through success scripts—and see the unbelievable results play out before you—to easily overcome potential objections. When you know the criteria your prospect uses to make decisions, it's a snap to identify additional advantages to using your product or service. This process shows you that you plan to succeed when you leave nothing to chance.

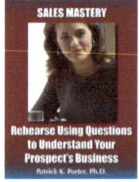

SM08 - Fill the Need, Close the Sale

Follow along as Dr. Patrick Porter shows you how to use this unique questioning approach. You'll learn to quickly break the trust barrier and discover your prospect's needs. Once you know your prospect's needs and values, closing the sale is as easy as taking a breath of fresh air!

SM09 - Eliminate Objections and Make the Sale

Your greatest sales obstacle lies in the mind of your prospect. This creative visualization process trains your brain to listen for and overcome objections—before your prospects know they have them! Selling is easy when you use the simple laws of persuasion.

SM10 - Remove Your Competition
from the Mind of Your Prospect

Your prospect has many options in the marketplace, and your job is to show them you're the best choice. Now, you can get your prospect to eliminate your competition from contention—without you using a single negative word against them. It's easier than you think when you use these four simple steps!

SM11 - Going with the Flow: Closing Strategies
& Objection Prevention

This refreshing process by Dr. Patrick Porter allows you to remove the stress of closing the deal. Objections are part of the sales game, but you'll learn how the power of "no" can actually help you reach your sales goals. By using this simple three-step process, you'll be ready and able to close the most difficult prospect. Master your mental state, and you'll master any sales situation.

SM12 - Using Sales Reframes
for Fun & Profit

Learn how to transition, or reframe, a negative statement into a positive one with this motivating session. Even the most difficult sale is easy when you can turn resistance into cooperation. Master the pre-frame and reframe and you'll help your prospects sell themselves!

SM13 - Tai Chi for the Sales Mind

Harmony is one of the most powerful forces in the universe. Your own negative thoughts work against you and harmfully affect your sales performance. When you use this inspirational technique, you will elevate your thoughts to the highest level without stress or struggle. When your mind is on your side, anything is possible!

PorterVision's Product Resources

Smoking Cessation Series
Patrick K. Porter, Ph.D.

Kicking your smoking habit doesn't get any easier or more fun than this! When you use Dr. Patrick Porter's proven strategies, you'll find that making this life-saving change comes about simply and effortlessly. With the new science of *creative visualization and relaxation* (CVR), you will extinguish the stress and frustration associated with quitting smoking, and you'll conquer your cravings like the tens of thousands of others who have used his processes.

You will learn to stay calm so you can easily and comfortably vanquish the old urge for cigarettes. Breaking the chains that have bound you to cigarettes has never been easier—now that you have made the choice to live your life tobacco-free and to start living the life of your dreams!

SS01 - Making the Decision To Be A Non-Smoker

Have you always wanted to quit smoking, but never had the confidence to take that plunge? With this CVR session, you'll learn about the cleansing power of you own mind, and use it to take a "mental shower" that will wipe away all thoughts of tobacco. With this process, you'll gladly make the decision to be tobacco-free for life!

SS02 - Making Peace With Your Mind

In this powerful creative session, Dr. Patrick Porter will show you that, while you once had a positive intention for having tobacco in your life, you no longer need it to live the life you desire. The smoker of the past will make peace with the clean air breather of the future in order to create a new, vibrant you! This mind-blowing technique will allow you to learn from your past, master your present, and accomplish all your future goals.

SS03 - Plan Your Life As A Non-Smoker

Every goal needs a plan, and in this process, Dr. Patrick Porter will guide you in visualizing and working a plan for your tobacco-free life. This motivational session will allow you to remember to forget cigarettes forever. You'll awake convinced being a nonsmoker is as easy as taking a breath of fresh air!

SS04 - Freedom From Tobacco At Work

You will get a handle on negative emotions such as anger, stress, and frustration. At the same time, you'll release any triggers that could potentially cause you to return to the old unwanted behavior. This process is specifically designed to help you learn new ways to handle daily breaks, drive time, and times when your co-workers might be smoking around you. Imagine the power of saying with a smile, "No, thanks, I am a non-smoker!"

SS05 - Craving-Free/Tobacco-Free

Dr. Patrick Porter will help you learn effective new ways for releasing the chains that have bound you to the habit of smoking. When you think like a "non-smoker" you will find it easy to remain free from tobacco even while driving, when walking out of smoke-free buildings, or after dinner. Cravings will become a thing of the past as you employ the world's greatest computer… your human mind!

SS06 - Rid Your Mind of Stress & Frustration

Imagine learning exciting new ways to rid yourself of the two main foes that have prevented you in the past from being tobacco-free forever. Dr. Patrick Porter has trained thousands to use these success strategies to eliminate stress and frustration, and now he is going to help you. When you use the power of your mind, it becomes easy to handle even the most difficult situations.

PorterVision Product Catalog

SS07 - Feel the Flow and Let Go - Tobacco-Free
You will tap into that innate intelligence that is greater than your conscious mind and release any anger that in the past may have driven you back to the smoking habit. With this process, you will learn visualization techniques of self-discipline and self-confidence that will train you to remain 100% tobacco-free for the rest of your life.

SS08 - Count Down to Being Tobacco-Free
During this creative visualization process, Dr. Patrick Porter will train you in techniques that will have you creating new triggers for health. As you develop self-discipline and self-confidence you will find the old negative triggers disappearing while a new life filled with health and abundance becomes yours.
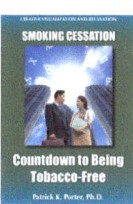

SS09 - Total Relaxation For The Non-Smoker
Relaxation is the key to transforming your new thoughts into action. Dr. Patrick Porter will help you gain the tools you need to be a non-smoker in day-to-day life. Best of all you will use the power of relaxation to transform stress into positive energy that will help you accomplish your goals. It is easy when you use your mind to simply relax away your cravings!

SS10 - Thinking Like A Non-Smoker
"Non-Smokers" think differently and you will learn how they avoid the usual quitting traps. With this breakthrough insight you will find it easy to remove the unwanted thoughts of tobacco forever. All permanent change starts in the mind and as you allow your mind to return to its natural way of thinking it will be as natural as your heart beat to remain tobacco-free.

SS11 – So Hum Tobacco-Free
Dr. Patrick Porter will train you to change your thoughts as easily as changing the channel on your television. With this breathing technique and creative visualization you will discover the power of selective thinking so you can remove your cravings and accentuate the positive of living tobacco-free. You will notice that energy flows where attention goes. As you place your attention on health and positive living, the unseen forces of your mind will support you in making this change permanent.

SS12 - Problem Solving As A Non-Smoker
Stress is one of the main reasons people smoke. In this creative visualization process, Dr. Patrick Porter trains you to creatively handle stress and create solutions in your life—solutions that will make it easy to stay tobacco-free. Once you learn these powerful techniques, you will use them in other areas of your life to become a conscious creator so you can accomplish each and every one of your goals.

SS13 - Healthy Mind For A Tobacco-Free Lifestyle
Dr. Patrick Porter will teach you a quick three-step process for thinking and acting healthfully. When you create your perfect place of relaxation, de-stressing and conquering deadly habits like smoking is easy. After that, you can focus the power of possibility thinking on other goals you have for your for life!

PorterVision's Product Resources

SportZone™ Series
Patrick K. Porter, Ph.D.

Success in sports is about being the best you can be, and visualization plays a key role in getting there. Why is visualization so important? Because you get what you rehearse in life, but that's not always what you want or intend. This is especially true when you are facing the pressures of athletics. The SportZone program is designed to help you tap into the mind's potential and make your sport of choice fun and enjoyable while taking your game to the next level. Visualization for sports performance is nothing new to top competitors—athletes from Tiger Woods to diver Greg Louganis and a variety of Olympians have used visualization to bring about optimal performance, overcome self-doubt, and give themselves a seemingly unfair advantage over their competition. Now the SportZone series can work for any athlete, from junior competitors to weekend enthusiasts. Yes, you can get more out of your sport and, in the process, get more out of life.

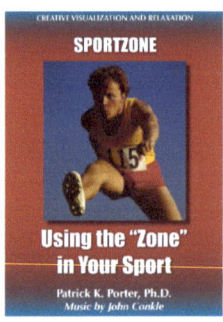

SZ01 – Using the "Zone" in Your Sport

When competitive athletes slip into their "zone" everything seems to work just right. Dr. Patrick Porter will help you get to that place where everything comes together. With this process you'll learn to put yourself into a state of "flow," your own personal "zone," so you can stay on top of your game. The "zone" is as easy to access as a deep breath once you have mastered the mental keys.

SZ02 – Control Your Emotions and Master Your Sport

It has been said that he or she who angers you conquers you; this is true even if the person who angers you *is you*! With this process you will learn a powerful self-visualization technique for keeping your emotions under control. With this easy technique you will no longer be giving away your power to others and will stop letting anger and frustration get the better of you.

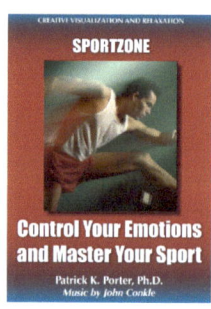

SZ03 – Super-Charge Your Self-Confidence

What would happen if you could cast out all doubt about your success? You would no longer *hope*, or *believe*, or *wish* it to be so—you would *know* it to be so! What if you could rid yourself of all doubt by simply changing your personal history (or at least your perception of it) and developing positive self-talk? You would super-charge your self-confidence, right? Well, that is exactly what you will learn with this process.

SZ04 – Psych Yourself Up! – and Perform Your Best Under Pressure

With this session Dr. Porter will help you to gain the courage to win. This may sound simple but what separates the best from the rest is mental toughness. You will be given the specific step-by-step strategies you need to perform your best under pressure now. Your success starts by eliminating "outcome anxiety" and ends with your willingness to visualize success.

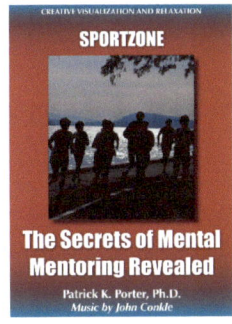

SZ05 – The Secrets of Mental Mentoring Revealed!

Everyone has an inner champion. With this breakthrough technique you will awaken yours and train it to go to work for you round the clock. Soon your other-than-conscious mind will be finding solutions and achieving goals even while you work, play, and sleep!

SZ06 – Set Goals Like the Pros

In this process Dr. Patrick Porter teaches you the secrets of full-sensory goal setting. You will develop the concentration to focus on daily, weekly and monthly goals and develop such self-discipline that others will be amazed at your determination.

SZ07 – Feel the Pressure and Win!

Whether you perform well under pressure or not, in this process Dr. Patrick Porter will help you learn ways to transform negative pressure into an iron will. Your other-than-conscious will then use that newfound inner strength to create results for you in sports and in life. Imagine how your body will respond when you train your brain to cast out doubt and step into the "zone" where success comes to you easily.

SZ08 – Build Desire, Drive & Perseverance

In this process you will learn how to create a compelling future and then draw that future to you like a powerful magnet. You will mentally train yourself to generate resources where and when you need them the most whether it's on the tee-box, a tennis court, a football field, or in your own backyard.

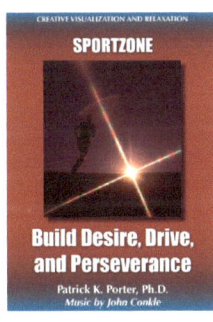

SZ09 – Think Like a Champion

Have you ever wondered how champions think? What goes through their minds just before a game-winning field goal or a high stakes putt? In this process Dr. Patrick Porter will reveal all the leadership skills of a professional athlete so you, too, can have the confidence and determination you need when you need it the most.

SZ10 - Lessons in Sports, Lessons in Life

Dr. Patrick Porter will help you design your own creativity generator. You will build problem-solving skills, work through specific scenarios, and see yourself achieving every one of your life goals. You will use the mental toughness developed in your sport to gain that same edge in your personal life.

Stress-Free Childbirth
Patrick K. Porter, Ph.D.

Bringing a child into the world should be an amazing life experience. Sadly, for many women, the joy of the event is lost due to fear, stress and pain. Also, research has shown that a fetus can actually feel the stress, worry, and negative emotions of the mother during pregnancy. Fortunately, with the discovery of the mind/body connection, women have an alternative—creative visualization and relaxation (CVR). This breakthrough series by PureCreation is designed to help the mother-to-be to relax, let go of stress, and enjoy the entire process of pregnancy, delivery and motherhood. In addition, the listener is taught to use the power of thought to create an anaesthetized feeling that can transform pain into pressure throughout labor and delivery—making the entire process stress-free for the entire family.

CB01 - Visualize and Realize Your Pregnancy Goals

Patrick K. Porter, Ph.D. will take you on a journey of the imagination where you'll train your brain to stay focused and on task. With this process, you'll start experiencing the relaxation response, set healthy priorities, and prepare your body for the many changes it will go through for the next nine months and beyond. This is the foundation session for the complete Stress-Free Childbirth program.

CB02 - Mental Skills for Pregnancy and Delivery

With this session negative thinking melts away and a calm state of emotional readiness replaces fear. The power of positive expectancy will lead you to positive results. Once you experience this mental training, and gain the relaxed mindset and inner confidence you need for motherhood, others may actually look to you for support!

CB03 - Stress-Free Pregnancy By Design

Dr. Patrick Porter will help you learn healthy ways to manage the stress of pregnancy. In this session you'll feel your worry melt away as you experience deep relaxation. There is nothing like the joy you'll feel when you start using your mind power to create a healthy environment for your newborn and you.

CB04 - Healthy Baby / Stress-Free Lifestyle

Concentration and focus are skills you'll need to experience a natural stress-free delivery. In this process, Dr. Porter will start your training in creating that anesthetized state whenever and wherever you need it. You'll feel your confidence soaring as you look forward to putting your newfound skills to work on your delivery date.

CB05 - Emotional Readiness Mental Toughness

Relax and allow your mind to build optimistic thinking during this life transition. You need only sit back, relax and watch anxiety melt away as you focus on health and wellbeing. Soon you'll notice how your confidence is growing as your baby grows. You'll build the mental toughness to convert fear into relaxation, preparing you for a memorable stress-free delivery.

CB06 - Balancing Your Life During Pregnancy

In today's world life comes at you fast. That doesn't change during pregnancy. You still have bills, housekeeping, errands, and traffic. Learn to let go of the stress and internal conflict associated with day-to-day living. You'll gain an inner serenity as you build new life skills just as surely as you are building a new life inside of you.

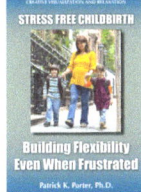
CB07 - Building Flexibility Even When Frustrated

Frustration is a given during pregnancy, and who can blame you? Your hormones are raging, your belly is swelling, and you have a dramatic life change ahead of you. With this process you'll train your body to relax and go with the flow. You'll master open and clear communication so that your entire family can be a part of your pregnancy. And, you'll focus on your health and the health of your baby.

CB08 – Building Your Delivery Team

Your mind is your best labor coach. After all, who knows what you need better than you? Now the skill of positive assertiveness can be yours. You'll know how and when to ask your family or your health care team for encouragement and support, and you'll master a breathing and relaxation technique to combat any discomfort. This process will also give you an opportunity to mentally rehearse the methods you learned in whatever birthing classes you've chosen.

CB09 – Going With the Flow …
Transforming Contractions To Pressure

Mentally prepare yourself for the last stage of pregnancy—labor and delivery. Learn how to manage your contractions as they increase in strength and frequency so you'll remain calm and breathe properly during and between contractions. Dr. Porter will help you plan for when your contractions reach peak intensity so that, with the power of your mind, you can feel only pressure and keep your body as stress-free as possible.

CB10 – Quick Tricks For Stress-Free Delivery

By using one of Dr. Porter's favorite CVR processes, you'll be ready to manage every aspect of your delivery. You'll focus on a safe, natural childbirth. And, best of all, with this mental exercise, you'll discover the keys to using your mind to accomplish your loftiest goals for motherhood and for life.

CB11 – Preparing for Motherhood

A new world awaits you after the stress-free delivery of your child. With this process, you'll be mentally, physically and emotionally prepared for motherhood. You'll discover ways to visualize solutions to problems you have not yet faced, so that even with a brand new person demanding nearly all of your attention, you can build a sense of balance back into your life.

CB12 - Enjoying Life after Pregnancy

Research shows that 20% of new moms experience postpartum depression. Dr. Porter will help you control the mood swings, anxiety, guilt, and persistent sadness that sometimes appear after childbirth. This process is to be used after the birth and can benefit a new mom for up to four months. Throughout the process you'll mentally rehearse your new lifestyle with joy and happiness for the entire family.

CB13 – Weight Loss and the New Mother

Once the new bundle has arrived and time commitments have changed, it's easy for a new mom to make her needs secondary to those of her family. You will discover easy tools to manage time and make your health and the health of your baby a top priority. Eating healthy has never been easier when you learn to use the power of your mind. Now there is no reason to hold on to that baby fat. You can lose all the weight you want naturally and healthfully.

Stress-Free Dentistry Series
Patrick K. Porter, Ph.D.

Whether you are someone who gets sweaty palms at the thought of a dentist's drill, hyperventilates the moment you lay eyes on a dental syringe, or simply gets butterflies in your stomach before going to the dentist, this program can benefit you. Studies show that over 40% of all people have a fear of dentistry. Other research demonstrates that having poor oral health can decrease your life expectancy by five years. Fear of the dentist can have many causes, some of which are objective, and others of which are subjective. For example, if you once experienced a great deal of pain while having a tooth pulled, the next time you need an extraction, you will likely be fearful because of your previous experience. This is subjective fear. On the other hand, if you later told a friend about your bad experience, and he subsequently became fearful when faced with a tooth extraction, this would be subjective fear.

Fear in and of itself is not bad. We are all born with certain fears that protect us, such as the fear of falling and the fear of loud noises. Fear stops us from doing dangerous things. The purpose of this series is to put fear in its proper perspective so that you can have a relaxed experience at every dental visit and enjoy the benefits of having healthy teeth and gums.

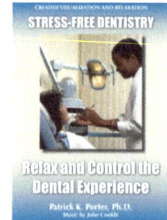

SFD01 - Relax and Control the Dental Experience

Allowing thoughts to control your emotions is a normal human experience. In this process, Dr. Patrick Porter will help you reverse this tendency, so you can control your emotions and stop reacting to negative thoughts. You will learn a simple yet powerful technique that will have you visualizing a pleasant visit to your dentist's office. You will also be guided through a process of releasing any emotions you may have tied to negative personal history experiences with dental or medical procedures

SFD02 - Mental Rehearsal for Instant Relaxation

Developing coping skills is a key element to overcoming your fear of dentistry. With this relaxing process, Dr. Patrick Porter will teach you to use a distraction technique that will eliminate anxiety and fear. Dentistry may not ever be fun for you, but it can be a relaxed and comfortable experience as you master these visualization techniques.

SFD03 – Eliminate False Beliefs & Build Self-Confidence

In this process you will explore beliefs about dentistry and eliminate those that are impacting you negatively. You will build the self-confidence necessary to comfortably handle any dental appointment, whether it be a cleaning, filling, or a more complex procedure. With these blocks gone, who knows, you might even enjoy your next dental experience!

SFD04 – Setting Expectations & Eliminating Dental Anxiety

Anxious reactions are natural whenever we face the unknown. In this visualization, Dr. Patrick Porter will be guiding you through processes that quickly build your self-esteem, enhance your assertiveness, and have you acting as your own advocate, asking the right questions so you understand even the most complex procedure.

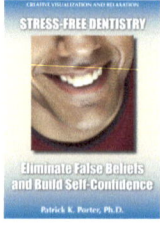

SFD05 - Control What You Think and Feel

Since energy always follows thought, in this creative visualization you will master the art of singular thinking. This will allow you to create a state of relaxation where you can control the sensations in your body by controlling your thoughts. It's easier than you think to control your dental experience, and certainly worthwhile so you'll have a lifetime of healthy teeth and gums.

Stress Reduction Series
Patrick K. Porter, Ph.D.

Stress is the most pervasive malady of our time. The effects on our health, productivity and quality of life are more devastating than most people care to admit. Luckily, you've just found the solution! CVR can help you see yourself as the healthy, happy, optimistic person you'd prefer to be. With this new image, your fears and frustrations fade away, your anxiety vanishes, and you no longer let small things stress you.

SR01 - Create Your Enchanted Forest for Stress Reduction
Follow along as Dr. Patrick Porter guides you through your personal enchanted forest—a quiet, serene place where you have nothing to do but relax. Your other-than-conscious mind will massage away all tension, allowing you to release all negative thoughts and feelings. You'll return from your magical forest filled with positive feelings, able to enjoy and express your true inner peace.

SR02 - Create Your Mountaintop Retreat for Stress Reduction

Say goodbye to all stress and confusion as you take a trip to this breathtaking mountaintop retreat. When you listen to this restful process, using your mind to relax your body will become as comfortable and automatic as breathing. The stress, strain and confusion of everyday life will melt away as you awake refreshed, revitalized and renewed!

SR03 - Experience Dream-time and Achieve Your Goals
Possibilities are limitless in your dreams! In this CVR session by Dr. Patrick Porter, you'll walk along your dream beach, leaving behind all stress, worry and tension. During your dreamtime, you'll be able to change past failures into triumphs—even meet your future self to see the successes you've achieved. You'll use your dreams to develop hidden talents, skills and abilities, and awaken convinced that infinite success will be yours.

SR04 - Putting Future Events Into Perspective

Research has proven that 97% of what we worry about never happens in the way we fear. With this powerful visualization, Dr. Patrick Porter will show you the benefits of having a healthy picture of the future. You will be amazed by what you can do when you learn to magnify positive thoughts. You'll put your future into perspective and learn creative ways to live your life without unhealthy stress. Your future will become bright and compelling as you take an active part in planning your personal success.

SR05 - Reducing Uncertainty And Doubt
When you cast out doubt, all that can remain is the truth—and the truth is you are more capable than you have been led to believe. Dr. Patrick Porter will guide you on the road to discovering hidden talents that will help you reduce or eliminate doubt. Just as a sponge absorbs water, so too your mind will soak up these soothing visualizations and train your brain to yield spontaneous relaxation, helping you to create a dynamically healthy body.

SR06 - Eliminating Negative Thinking

Research has proven that negative thinking has a chemically negative effect on the body. With this visualization, Dr. Patrick Porter will help you to experience the healing force of your mind. Once your own healing power is working within your body, you will build a shield of protection against anything that is less than vibrant health for you. It will become second nature to eliminate negative thoughts as you enjoy the energy of positive thoughts and actions.

PorterVision's Product Resources

SR07 - Making Peace With Your Past

Your past works as a filter helping you make decisions about the present and the future. When you release the emotional baggage that is holding you back from a true commitment to healthy living, attaining optimum health becomes easy. Dr. Patrick Porter will teach you to forgive, forget, and move on with a healthy body and attitude. With the power of forgiveness on your side, the unseen forces of your mind will go to work creating radiant health.

SR08 - Rehearse Mental Harmony for Physical Health

Dr. Porter will guide you through mental rehearsal for setting and accomplishing your health goals. With this powerful process you will actively use mental housecleaning techniques to cleanse your mind of negative beliefs from your past, and then help you to unleash your body's natural ability to create perfect health.

SR09 - Stress-free Mind, Healthy Body

You will enjoy learning how everything starts with a thought and then becomes a thing. In much the same way as your shadow reflects your physical form, your thoughts, actions and beliefs shape your body. Sit back, relax and enjoy discovering these amazing secrets for cultivating a healthy mind and enjoying life in a dynamically healthy, strong body.

SR10 - Developing Spontaneous Relaxation

Sometimes you need to relax and get focused right now! During this session, Dr. Patrick Porter will train your other-than-conscious mind to soak up a series of soothing creative visualization and relaxation processes, and train your brain to yield relaxed and positive thoughts on demand.

SR11 - Free Your Mind & Experience Your Healthy Body

We think thousands of thoughts every day. Learn how to cast out the negative, listen to the positive, and unleash your mind's healing force. You will build a shield of protection against anything that might stop you from experiencing radiant good health.

SR12 - Creating a Life of Vibrant Health

You will learn how easy it is to release any hurts from your past that might holding you back from your commitment to health. This process engages the healing graces that allow you to forgive, forget, and move on with a healthy body and attitude.

SR13 - Allowing a Life of Health & Abundance

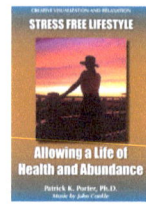

Some people think they need stress to be motivated. In this session, you will learn to use positive motivators to get what you want. You will be guided through the garden in your mind where you will train your other-than-conscious to focus on action, success, and health. Working with the healing intelligence of the body has never been easier as you learn new and creative ways to live your life without the need for stress.

Vibrant Health Series
Patrick K. Porter, Ph.D.

Of all the cells in your body, more than 50,000 will die and be replaced with new cells, all in the time it took you to read this sentence! Your body is the vehicle you have been given for the journey of your life. How you treat your body determines how it will treat you. Dr. Patrick Porter (PhD) will show you how, by using creative visualization and relaxation (CVR), you can recharge and energize your body, mind, and spirit. This series is for people who are looking for more than good health; it's for those who will settle for nothing less than vibrant health!

VH01 Staying Focused in the Present

Your emotions can either help your body stay healthy, or they can be the cause of disease. Negative feelings such as regret, worry, or anxiety about an upcoming event not only a waste your precious life, but also add stress to the body, which makes you more susceptible to disease. In this CVR process, Dr. Porter will help you stay present and focused on the beauty of each moment.

VH02 Visualize a Heart-Healthy Lifestyle

Heart disease is not a male issue alone; it is the top killer of American women. To protect your heart, you need a plan that includes movement, a healthy diet, and a positive mental attitude. You use an average of forty-three muscles to frown and only seventeen muscles to smile. You'll find smiling even easier now that you are taking an active roll in protecting the health of your heart.

VH03 Exercise—Just Do It!

Did you know that our human bodies recreate our skeletons every three months, we get an entirely new skin each and every month, and our bodies are brand new within two years? This means that the only thing getting older is our thoughts. Exercise is proven to help you live a longer, happier, and healthier life.

VH04 Unlocking the Healing Force of Positive Thoughts

You are what you think about all day long. If you want to feel and look great, monitor your thoughts closely to ensure that you are thinking only positive, forward-moving thoughts. Dr. Porter will teach you a visualization technique that will help you catch negative thoughts before they can harm you and then turn those thoughts around into a positive affirmation.

VH05 Planning a Healthy Diet for Vibrant Health

How do you think your life would change if fresh, healthy, and live foods were the foods you craved? In this process, you will visualize a healthy lifestyle where the live foods are appealing to you, and the processed and fast foods are a big turn-off. Health care practitioners will tell you that you have to provide your physical body with high quality fuel if you want it to run properly.

PorterVision's Product Resources

VH06 Train Your Brain to Give You Adequate Rest

During this CVR session, Dr. Porter will teach you to move through the wide-awake state of beta, into the relaxation state known as alpha, and then into the creative state know as theta. From here you will easily train your brain to provide you uninterrupted sleep. Science has shown that for sleep to be healing and rejuvenating, you need to engage the REM pattern. REM sleep is your nervous system's way of healing and refueling your body.

VH07 Problem Solving For Vibrant Health

A sharp mind is essential to optimum brain health, and mental exercise and brain stimulation are the keys to maintaining an active mind. The brain creates unhealthy neuro-chemicals whenever you are focused on problems. By placing your attention on solutions, you encourage your brain to create the healthy neuro-chemicals that make you feel good.

VH08 Supercharge Your Memory & Concentration

Dr. Porter will teach you simple tips for improving your everyday memory of names, addresses, events, and whatever else you wish to remember. You will gain confidence in knowing that your memory is getting stronger and your brain is staying healthy as you move through this journey we call life.

VH09 Surround Yourself With a Great Support System

Whether family, friends or coworkers, the company you keep plays a key roll in the health of your mind and body. Dr. Porter will give you tactful ways to keep yourself surrounded from every side with positive-minded, healthy people who are on your team—people who will care for, support, love, respect, and appreciate you as you reach your goal of vibrant health.

Wealth Consciousness Series

Inspired by the principles of Napoleon Hill's Think and Grow Rich.

"Imagination is the workshop of your mind, capable of turning mind energy into accomplishment and wealth." – Napoleon Hill

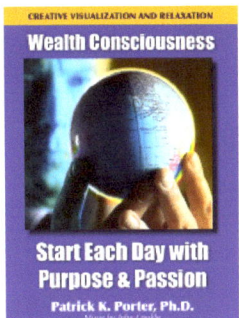

WC01 START EACH DAY WITH PURPOSE AND PASSION

Successful people have what Napoleon Hill called "mind energy," on their side. Dr. Patrick Porter will guide you in using this power of intention to focus your imagination on the success and prosperity you desire.

WC02 COMMIT TO A LIFE SPENT WITH LIKE-MINDED PEOPLE

Together with Dr. Patrick Porter, you will activate what Napoleon Hill termed the "third mind," or group intelligence. With each visit to this level of the mind, your mastermind alignment will grow stronger.

WC03 TRUST THE POWER OF INFINITE INTELLIGENCE

Do you sometimes feel as though fear of poverty has control over you? During this CVR session, you will visualize and realize the thoughts and actions that bring wealth and riches into your life.

WC04 EXCEED EXPECTATIONS —SERVE OTHERS, SERVE YOURSELF

Imagine awakening each day aware that every seed you sow will come back to you as overwhelming abundance. In this session, you will become motivated by a help others mind-set. This feeling of service will magnetize wealth and abundance to you.

WC05 TRANSMIT A PLEASING PERSONALITY TO THE WORLD

How might other people respond to you if you radiated enthusiasm? During this creative-visualization process, the radiant light that is your true personality will be invited out for all to see. It's easy to draw wealth and abundance to you when you show up with a pleasing personality.

WC06 HARNESS THE POWER OF PERSONAL INITIATIVE

Self-motivated people tend to be the happiest and most successful. Starting with the first listening of this creative-visualization process, you will gain the behaviors of a self-starter. Each morning a newfound personal initiative will inspire you to greater success.

WC07 CLAIM YOUR RIGHT TO A POSITIVE MENTAL ATTITUDE

The greatest riches in the world come from the heart. From your heart you will uncover the positive attitude that resides in that place where you dream. You will eliminate unproductive thoughts, enhance your relationships, balance your life, and make your dreams come true

WC08 RADIATE ENTHUSIASM—YOUR KEY TO SUCCESS CONSCIOUSNESS

Desire creates enthusiasm, which fuels determination and leads to success. During this visualization you will tap your "pulsating desire" to win—that wellspring of physical energy that we call enthusiasm.

WC09 GRASP THE POWER OF THOUGHT AND ORDAIN YOUR DESTINY

In this visualization you will harness self-discipline, which Napoleon Hill called, "taking possession of one's mind." This new habit will stoke the inner fire that ordains your destiny. Get ready to take charge of your life as your positive new thoughts create a new world around you.

WC10 TUNE INTO INFINITE INTELLIGENCE FOR ACCURATE THINKING

During this visualization, you will learn to trust your connection with infinite intelligence just as other accurate thinkers do—by thinking for yourself. This process will give you the time to examine information, build discernment, and make the decisions that shape your destiny.

WC11 AWAKEN THE SEEDS OF ACHIEVEMENT

Now you can arouse the sleeping seeds of greatness that will carry you to heights you might never have dreamed possible. The key to this process is controlled attention. By learning to fix your attention on what you want, instead of what you don't want, prosperity and harmony will be the natural byproduct.

WC12 HARNESS THE POWER OF COOPERATIVE EFFORT

During this visualization, you will move beyond mastermind groups into a coordinated effort to work with a team spirit that includes definiteness of purpose and absolute harmony.

WC13 FIND THE SOLUTION TO ANY PROBLEM

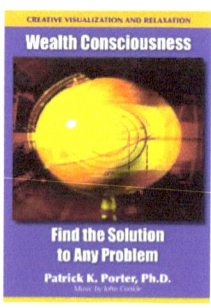

Albert Einstein was fond of saying, "You can never solve a problem on the level at which it was created." What Einstein understood is the power within the other-than-conscious mind to dwell on solutions instead of problems. Soon you will see problems for what they really are—temporary setbacks and stepping stones to success.

WC14 TAP INTO THE CREATIVE VISION OF INFINITE INTELLIGENCE

Wealth streams to those who work smarter not harder. In this creative visualization you will make the inner connection with the guiding force that lets you accomplish the impossible. Through this inner faith the path to wealth is illuminated.

WC15 HEALTH CONSCIOUSNESS, WEALTH CONSCIOUSNESS

There is a universal truth that what the mind dreams about the body brings about. Balance in mind and body is key to wealth consciousness. In this process, you will plan a life of wealth, health, and abundance from the inside out.

WC16 EMPLOY THE POWER OF TIME FOR WEALTH CONSCIOUSNESS

In this program you will discover how the captains of industry used assertiveness and diplomacy to get what they want. You will keep the dream stealers and time bandits out of your life so you can keep your eye on the prize and enjoy the ride to riches.

WC17 BUILD YOUR WEALTH ONE HABIT AT A TIME

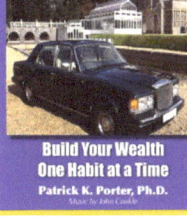

Just as nature adheres to strict laws, the person of wealth lives by the laws of excellence. Making positive choices becomes a driving power in your life as you master the power of thought. Your other-then-conscious mind will become your guide in building unlimited wealth.

PorterVision's Product Resources

Weight Loss Series
Patrick K. Porter, Ph.D.

Now you can design the body you want and the life you love. That's right, you can have the trim, healthy body you've always dreamed of by simply changing the way you see yourself and your life. Once you have a new image of yourself, everything else changes—junk food and fast food lose their appeal, healthy foods become desirable, and you eat only when you're hungry. With the this System you will overcome common weight loss mistakes, learn to eat and think like a naturally thin person, conquer cravings, and increase your self-confidence. Each week you will take another step toward a lifetime of healthy living; losing weight is the natural by product of these changes. While the average diet lasts just 72 hours and focuses on depriving you of the foods you love, Dr. Patrick Porter supercharges your weight loss motivation with these powerful *creative visualization and relaxation* processes! You will eliminate the problem where it started—*your own mind.* There is simply no easier way to lose weight than CVR!

WL01 - Safely Speeding Up Weight Loss
In this powerful process, you'll learn to safely speed up weight loss by thinking, acting and responding like a naturally thin person. Your sense of worth will improve when you discover and use inner resources you never even knew you had. Sit back, relax, and discover how easy it is to turn your body into a fat-burning machine—and keep the weight off forever!

WL02 - Simple Steps for Self-Confidence for Weight Control

When you learn these simple steps for self-confidence, you will unleash your creative mind, allowing your mind and body to work together for lasting weight loss. Dr. Patrick Porter will help you discover your own bright and compelling future—a future where all your physical, mental and emotional goals have been reached. You'll awaken with complete confidence in your new, healthy behaviors, aware that your future is filled with infinite possibilities!

WL03 - Eliminate the Gain/Loss Cycle
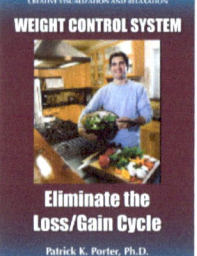
End your yo-yo dieting cycle! With this motivational CVR process, you'll let go of the past, because the past no longer controls you. The present is your most powerful moment, and in the present you're free to make the choices that will help you realize and maintain your natural and ideal weight forever.

WL04 - Producing Success One Thought at a Time

Every day, thoughts move through your mind, many without your awareness.
In this session, Dr. Patrick Porter helps you eliminate the negative thoughts, patterns and beliefs that have been keeping you from reaching your goals. As you release negative thoughts—and excess weight—you'll free yourself to enjoy more joy and success than you ever thought possible!

WL05 - Sunrise Agreement
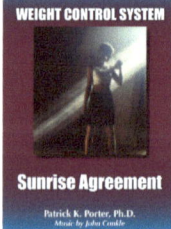
As you experience this dynamic process by Dr. Patrick Porter, your old habits and new desires will communicate and create a contract for success. With this "Sunrise Agreement," you'll awaken knowing every day is a new day, given to you to create the changes you desire. Most of all, you'll experience every day with the power to use your mind and body to improve your life at the most powerful moment possible—now!

WL06 - Create Your Weight Loss Support Team

Support is an important the key to maintaining the results that will keep you naturally thin. With this visualization you will use the power of your mind to help you to build a caring and supportive team that will improve every relationship. With this type of attitude you will create all the support you need to reach your goals.

PorterVision Product Catalog

WL07 - Developing Positive Eating Patterns

Deep inside, your body knows what it needs to operate at its full, vibrant potential. With this session, you'll mentally journey back to a time when you enjoyed doing the best for your body. When you bring those skills back with you to the present, you'll find yourself more comfortable and confident each day, effortlessly eating the right foods at the right times. Above all, you'll know that appetite is of the mind, but hunger is of the body!

WL08 - Turn Up Your Fat-Burning Thermostat

Use Creative Visualization to rehearse proven steps that will allow your body to convert naturally into a fat burning machine. These simple tips will help to increase your metabolic rate and show you how to keep your weight off.

WL09 - Motivation for Monday Morning

In the past, Monday mornings have always seemed the ideal time to start changes in your life. The problem came when that Monday morning motivation faded throughout the week. With this inspiring process by Dr. Patrick Porter, you'll learn to recapture that beginning-of-the-week motivation and use it every day of the week. One day at a time, you'll know that every day, in every way, you're getting better and better at making the changes you desire.

WL10 - Using Your Mind's Eye for Weight-Loss Success

Enter the theater of your mind and watch your own weight-loss success take place before your eyes. Success will follow you as naturally as your shadow when you solve the problems of your past with solutions you see in your present and future. Most of all, you'll awaken a feeling of success in you today, knowing that the accomplishments you see in your mind's eye will happen in your body naturally, one day at a time.

WL11 - Stop Dieting and Start Living

Your mind has a natural ability for removing mental obstacles to your weight loss. You will discover why appetite is of the mind and hunger is of the body. Returning to your natural weight is easy when you plan a lifetime of healthy thoughts and actions.

WL12 - Exercising is Energizing

Wouldn't you love to have fun exercising? With this process by Dr. Patrick Porter, you'll develop the thoughts and skills of a person who naturally loves to exercise. You'll use your creative mind to imagine, and then do, physical activities you enjoy. When you're in complete, optimistic control of your mind and body, you'll see excellence in the naturally-thin people around you and develop the same abilities in your own life.

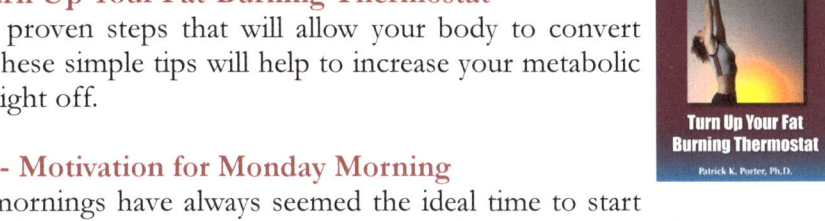

WL13 - Take Back Control of Your Appetite

The average person gains up to four pounds a year. That's a 40-pound weight gain in ten short years! This process is developed to break this cycle. You will be visualizing success by overcome any poor eating habits and associated stress. You will discover why true happiness starts when you eat to live… And eliminate any thought of living to eat!

WL14 - Break the Chains that Keep You from Ultimate Health

Break the bonds of the past that keep you tied to foods and habits that no longer serve you. With this process, you'll find it easy to create a new reality where you are no longer imprisoned by negative thoughts, patterns or beliefs. Instead, Dr. Patrick Porter will help you open the treasure chest of your natural talents skills and abilities, and awaken yourself to the freedom of today. Best of all, these changes will feel as simple as a walk on the beach!

PorterVision's Product Resources

WL15 - Stay Fit Through Healthy Eating Patterns

Your body image starts in your mind. Using your powerful subconscious mind you will unlock your unlimited potential! With this visualization you will eliminate the habits that caused you to gain weight and then choose the habits and behaviors you need to remain naturally thin for life. It's easy to stay on track when you forget about dieting and make simple lifestyle changes.

WL16 - Extinguish Junk Food Cravings

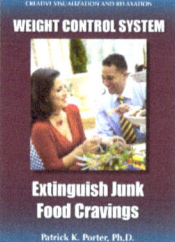

It's easy to relax and allow your mind to conquer the junk food habit. You'll visualize simple steps that end binge eating and transform your appetite so you'll crave the healthy foods that keep you thin. Imagine your joy when you feel confident at every meal. Using the power of your mind, you will take back control and leave your unhealthy eating patterns in the past.

WL17 - Quick Tips To Lose Weight Even If You Eat Out Everyday

Eating out can be a treat and a timesaver. Someone else does the cooking and there are no dishes to do. Now you can extend that joy by making healthy choices—even if your choice isn't on the menu. You will discover how to take back control of your health by taking control of your food choices. There's no reason you can't enjoy eating out with family and friends and still have a naturally thin body. It's simple when you plan success through the power of your other-than-conscious mind.

WL18 - Eliminate The Traps Associated With Dieting

Dieting traps can vary from Monday morning blues to Friday night fever—traps almost every dieter has fallen prey to. Now discover how easy it is to avoid these dieting traps by using your creative mind to rehearse all your best intentions. Soon you will find yourself demonstrating the skills of a naturally thin person no matter the weather, your mood, or the day of the week. When you choose to become a conscious creator in your weight loss journey, success becomes as natural as breathing.

WL19 - Visualize & Realize a Lifetime of Weight Loss Success

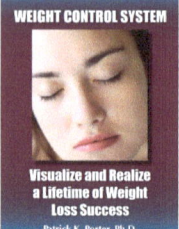

No one wants to have to diet over and over again. This session will reframe the old patterns that held you back in the past so you can lose your weight once and for all. You will make peace with your past, realizing that the past was a proving ground for the future. As you master the art of relaxation, you will instead visualize a lifetime of new behaviors that can be realized in a very effective, easy and fun way!

WL20 - Making the Connection for Permanent Weight Loss

You will use your mind to discover the secrets of naturally thin people and how to implement them in your life for permanent weight loss results. Once you know the truth, the dieting lie that chained you to overweight habits will melt away. With this connection, true health will be yours and negative thoughts about yourself will never again control you.

WL21 - Eliminate the Desire for Sugar & Chocolate

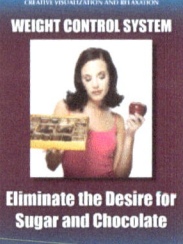

When you use your mind's natural abilities, eliminating your cravings for sweet, starchy and even fatty foods becomes completely painless. You will learn to focus on creating the desire for positive, life-giving foods that are fresh and alive. From this new mindset, you'll respond to foods with health in mind. You will explore the possibility that nothing taste as good as thin feels!

WL22 - Self Control And Radiant Health

When you learn to erase all doubt from your mind, it's easy to stay purposeful and on track with your health goals. Can you imagine how easy it would be to display discipline and confidence when it's enjoyable and fun? Well, that's exactly what Dr. Patrick Porter has done for you in this life-affirming session.

PorterVision Product Catalog

WL23 - Asking For What You Need and Getting What You Want

Do you know how to say no to people? Do you know how to ask for what your want? If' you've had trouble communicating your needs and wants in the past, it will become easy and automatic for you to achieve your success using these exciting new communication skills. You will visualize yourself communicating with others with assertiveness and confidence. As you use the laboratory of your mind to create powerful, fulfilling relationships, you will get more out of life and have fun in the process.

WL24 - Choosing Habits That Keep You Naturally-Thin

Unleash the power of selective thinking and learn to choose the foods and activities that are healthiest for your body. Eliminate the need for the dead, devitalized foods of the past as you remember . . . "Its not for me, but for my body, that I eat healthy foods." You will build a lifestyle that will support you in staying naturally thin.

WL25 - Exercise - Your Key To Lasting Health & Vitality

With this visualization you will ignite your enthusiasm for health and exercise. You will mentally rehearse your active new lifestyle where exercise is fun and enjoyable. Imagine how good you will feel as you burn fat, build muscle, and sculpt the body you want. Warning... using this process may transform your body into a fat burning machine!

WL26 - Breezing Through the Weekends Naturally Thin

With the average diet lasting only 72 hours—it starts on Monday and ends before Thursday— breezing through the weekends may seem like a tall order. But, now you can end the weekly weight loss roller coaster. This visualization is specially designed to keep your goals in high gear even on the weekend. Imagine the joy of starting the week with unlimited confidence!

WL27- Free Yourself from Overweight Thinking

As you develop your naturally thin mind-set, it's important to unlock the gates of your mind and release the past. Once you develop this new way of thinking, you free yourself from fat-induced discomfort. Dr. Patrick Porter will help you build your new body image; you'll envision the future where you are healthy, confident, slim and attractive.

WL28 - Make Exercise An Automatic Part Of Your Life

Studies show that people who learn to enjoy exercise are far more likely to maintain their weight loss. In this CVR session you will find powerful ways to boost your metabolism, which is your key to lasting energy. When exercise is automatic and fun you create a more active lifestyle.

WL29 - Sugar Busters … How to Have Your Sweets and Lose Weight, Too

Even naturally thin people eat sweets from time to time. Now you can, too— without guilt or shame. In this CVR session Dr. Patrick Porter will show you how you can occasionally eat sweets without derailing your weight loss by slowing down the insulin response and keeping your body in fat burning mode.

WL30 - Learn the 10 to 1 Method for Giving Your Body What It Needs

In this process you will start to learn to master CVR on your own. Imagine having instant triggers to help you throughout the day to think and eat like a naturally thin person. That is exactly what Dr. Patrick Porter guides you to do with this deeply relaxing visualization.

PorterVision's Product Resources

WL31 - Make Your Daily Activities Your Daily Motivation

During this process you will close your eyes, sit back, relax, and visualize how your daily routines can turn into excitement as you mentally cleanse your mind and body and discover the true you. By knowing what you want and following through—even when you don't want to—you build the habits of a naturally thin person.

WL32 - Make Your Motivation to Exercise Sizzle!

Exercise is fun when you feel motivated. Now you can get that edge with these creative tools that build your motivation and drive. While listening to this process you'll be guided to develop an effective and lasting exercise program. You'll be turning fat into lean body mass by using your mind to make exercise fun.

WL33 - Building Your Self-confidence and Self-esteem

If you've ever failed at dieting, you've lived the frustration and disappointment that follows. In this session Dr. Porter will help you erase all that negativity for good. You'll then discover fun and creative ways to accentuate the positive and transform your thoughts, actions and beliefs into those of a healthy, happy slim person.

WL34 - Unlocking Your Innate Intelligence to Re-create Your Body

Get ready to unlock the power of choice as you use your body's innate intelligence to stop the war within you. In this process, Dr. Porter will show you the difference between power and force. When you make peace with your body, you don't have to force it to do anything. You'll then find it easy to ride the power wave of change that will make it easy to think and eat the way thin people do.

WL35 - Using Assertiveness in Weight Control

It's easy to say *yes* or *no* when you are steadfastly focused on your health goals. Dr. Porter will help you experience progressive relaxation while you plan your life as a naturally thin person. Understanding the hidden secrets behind the power words of *yes* and *no* will set you free from the emotional roller coaster of the lose/gain cycle. Rehearsing when and where to use these power words will help you achieve your weight loss and health goals for life.

WL36 - Finding the Exercise You Like and the Time to Do It

Without proper motivation, the other-than-conscious mind can choose destructive or limiting behaviors that may sabotage your weight loss goals. During this process, Dr. Patrick Porter will help you design a healthy environment where exercise fits into a busy lifestyle. Learn to create balance in your home and work life so you'll be thinking and acting like a thin person in no time.

WL37 - Accept and Love Your Body

We tend to give the most attention to those we care about most. Now is the time to give your body the loving care it needs and deserves. When you learn to build a positive relationship with yourself by loving and accepting your body, making good choices becomes easy. Plus, all of your relationships will improve. It all starts with your thoughts.

WL38 - Gain Power Over Your Appetite

During this session, Dr. Porter will help you discover how *appetite is of the mind and true hunger is of the body*. You will learn to recognize the difference between appetite and hunger so you can make food choices from a place of self-empowerment. Soon you'll be eating only when you are truly hungry and automatically stopping when you are full. You'll experience the truth that power stems from choice, and you will choose to eat only what your body needs.

WL39 - Staying on Track with Your Transition to Thinness

PorterVision Product Catalog

Everyday you are bombarded with over 50,000 messages, each one prompting you to think or act in certain ways - no wonder staying focused can seem impossible! Dr. Porter will help you to get and stay focused on what's most important to you—your transition to a healthier, happier lifestyle.

WL40 - Eliminate Your Weight Loss Enemies For Good

During this visualization process, Dr. Porter will teach you to eliminate those old enemies that kept you trapped in the negative programming of the past. Whether it's food, family, friends, or your own self-talk, you will relax and allow your other-than-conscious mind to work out success on your terms.

WL41 - Plan a Healthy Home and Workplace

Now you can build the skills necessary for creating balance in your home, work, and personal life. These are the skills that will have you thinking and acting like a thin person for life. During this visualization, Dr. Patrick Porter will teach you proven ways to motivate yourself, to retrain the other-than-conscious mind, and to eliminate any destructive or limited behaviors that may otherwise sabotage your weight loss goals.

WL42 Super Charge Your Self-image

Your self-image is the way you think about yourself and it directly affects the food choices you make. With this CVR program, you will learn powerful techniques that empower you to enjoy fresh and alive foods as much or more than the old junk foods of the past. You will learn to savor the flavors in fresh, natural foods. You will also learn to take pleasure in the energy that you derive from the foods that promote lasting weight-loss results. And along the way you will be building a healthy image of yourself.

WL43 Eliminate Fear And Stay Naturally Thin

Dr. Porter will help you to eliminate fear-of-failure thinking, the primary factor in disappointing weight-loss results. Apply this powerful CVR process to program success at the deep other-than-conscious level of your mind. When you eliminate fear-of-failure thinking, keeping the weight off becomes effortless.

WL44 Mental Toughness for Weight Management

During this CVR program, you will create a rock-solid attitude about being naturally thin and staying at your natural and ideal weight. This process mentally trains you to generate resources where and when you need them to accomplish your health goals. With so many forces seeming to work against you, you will come to realize that your needs are just as important as everyone else's.

WL45 Increasing Self-Esteem and Optimism

Self-esteem is an inside job. In this session, you will learn to calm and steady your emotions simply by sitting back, relaxing, and enjoying the visualization sequence. You will create the habit of optimism, which will help you conquer fear, frustration, and anxiety while experiencing a peaceful mental vacation. With this overall feeling of wellbeing, you can easily accomplish your health and weight goals.

WL46 Conquering Cravings for Sugar and Unhealthy Fats

PorterVision's Product Resources

Use this powerful guided visualization process to help you eliminate those old enemies that kept you trapped in the lose/gain cycle. Whether your cravings are related to stress, hormones, habit, or your own self-talk, relax and allow your other-than-conscious mind to work out success on your terms.

WL47 Removing the Unwanted Appetite of the Past

Now you can harness the power of your mind to overcome any past programming. At the same time, you will learn to recognize true hunger, which is a different feeling from appetite. You will learn how to unlock the power of possibility thinking and feel the habits of a naturally thin person grow within you.

WL48 Healthy Eating During the Holidays

Recapture the joy of the holidays. Why suffer or feel deprived when everyone else is having a good time? When you focus your mind on the positive experiences, and easily eat and think like a naturally thin person, your holidays will be a delightful experience once again.

WL49 Put Your New Year's Resolutions on Overdrive

Tap into the limitless motivation of your other-than-conscious mind to stay on track, build unstoppable resolve, and accomplish your resolutions with ease. Watch the pounds disappear as your confidence builds and your life improves!

WL50 Giving Thanks and Staying Slim

Did you know the average person gains four pounds over the holidays? That's forty pounds in ten short years! You will be using this CVR process to eliminate Thanksgiving guilt. To create healthy holidays, this process takes you step-by-step through the season, helping you overcome the poor eating habits and associated stress. Eat less and enjoy the holidays more – you can't beat that combination!

WL51 Celebrating Parties and Picnics Guilt-Free

Why stress at parties while everyone else is having fun? Relax with this process and you'll soon find yourself enjoying good times with friends and family without the worry, deprivation, or guilt of the past.

WL52 Keeping It Off with a Naturally Thin Mind-set

Imagine your life after you find fun ways of focusing on yourself at your natural and healthy weight. Dr. Patrick Porter will help you discover how, by developing an awareness of who you truly are, it will be easy for you to eat, think, and respond as a naturally thin person. You will keep your focus on health, and your weight will take care of itself.

**For a complete list of
Creative Visualization & Relaxation (CVR)
Please go to www.PorterVision.com**

PorterVision Product Catalog

What the Media has to say about CVR . . .

By: **Anne-Marie Cook**
Spa **Magazine**

Health Report—Creative Visualization
Want to drop pounds, quit smoking, or stress less? Then consider guided visualization. A technique used by psychologists since the late 1800s, it is now being offered at spas, too—such as Mezzanine Spa in New York City and The TreeHouse in Venice Beach, California – through a program called Creative Visualization and Relaxation (CVR). The brainchild of Dr. Patrick Porter, CVR utilizes flashing LEDs and sound pulses to guide you into a relaxed state bordering on sleep in which suggestions reach deeper than they can when the mind is alert. During each of the more than 300 CVR programs available, you are asked to visualize yourself in various scenarios to train your mind to react to old triggers with new behaviors. There's also a personal version that lets you take the power of positive thinking with you wherever you go.

By: *Spirit of Women*
Spring 2008

Envision Yourself to Better Health
Guided imagery is similar to meditation, except that the focus of your thought is a physical part of the body you'd like to strengthen. The process of picturing a healthy heart or a svelte body can lower stress levels and help you "see" what it would feel like to be well.

High-tech Guided Imagery
You don't necessarily have to shell out big bucks for a personalized coach to reap the benefits of guided imagery . . . self-administered mental coaching programs can help you conquer bad habits or initiate good habits just by envisioning it—sitting back in your favorite easy chair, taking a deep breath, and completely relaxing every muscle in the body. A critical element . . . is light and sound technology to make your brain more receptive to the coaching. Just as the stimuli of music beats and flashing lights at a night club affect your brain . . . light and sound technology bring your brain frequency to a state called theta. The theta state is a meditative one that reportedly leads to higher levels of creativity, learning and inspiration.

The "Wellness Revolution" is Sweeping the Nation
Forward thinking hospitals that address patient demand for total wellness are now providing creative visualization and relaxation (CVR) mental coaching for their patients.

The Once-a-day Stress Relief Formula
"FOR ME AND ONLY ME"
Science proves that if you don't process your day-to-day experiences, they stay in your sub-conscious and keep you awake. Relaxation and exercise, yoga, music and the overall environment can help. It's getting back to the basics of the mind, body and spirit.
Dr. Patrick Porter explained that it's important to take a few minutes during the day to just unplug your phone and become consciously aware of your thoughts. If you slow down mentally, you become more

By: **Lenny LaCour**
PULSE **Magazine**

59

aware of your unconscious thinking. Basically, we clog up our minds to the point where we can't focus on positive thoughts. Porter's theory is that our mind works in blocks of information. The conscious mind can only store several chunks at a time, and the rest of the thoughts remain in the subconscious waiting to be resolved. It's important to clear your mind to allow the wind to blow the thoughts through.

Dr. Porter's program is based on creative visualization and relaxation (CVR). Sessions result in stress release, clearer thinking, improved memory and enhanced creativity—a spiritual journey within yourself indeed.

The New Generation of Mind-Body Therapies—Biofeedback and Brain Training

By: Chris Cunningham
Massage Magazine

Massage therapist Leslie White uses the biofeedin equipment and Dr. Patrick Porter's soothing voice to full advantage during her massage sessions. She said the combination of light, pulsating sound and "Dr. Porter's very pleasant voice softly saying, 'Now you will feel her hands massaging,'" really helps the clients "focus on themselves."

Meditation at the Mezzanine Spa

"After about 15 minutes, it was as though my mind and body were at one. It was similar to the feeling you get when you're almost asleep and then have a sort of "mini-dream" that brings you back to the waking world."

By: **Kelly Hushin**
BeautyNewsNYC.com

Researchers tested novice meditators on a button-pressing task requiring speed and concentration. Performance was greater after 40 minutes of meditation than after a 40-minute nap.

The Boston Globe
November 23, 2005

What the Research has to say about Frequency Following Response...

Dr. Roger K. Cady, Dr. Norman Shealy in "Neurochemical Responses to Cranial Electrical Stimulation and Photo-Stimulation via Brain Wave Synchronization." Study performed by the Shealy Institute of Comprehensive Health Care, Springfield, Missouri, 1990, 11 pp.:
Eleven patients had peridural and blood analysis performed before and after the relaxation sessions using flash emitting goggles. An average increase of beta-endorphin levels of 25% and serotonin levels of 21% were registered. The beta-endorphin levels are comparative to those obtained by cranial electrical stimulation (CES). This indicates a potential decrease of depression related symptoms when using photic stimulation.

Dr. Norman Shealy, Dr. Richard Cox In `Pain Reduction and Relaxation with Brain Wave Synchronization (Photo-Stimulation). Study performed by the Forest Institute of Professional Psychology, Springfield, Missouri, 1990, 9pp.
Cerebral synchronization was obtained with photic stimulation devices and tested on more than 5,000 patients suffering from chronic pain and stress-symptoms during the `80s. A detailed study on 92 patients indicated that 88 obtained relaxation results higher than 60% after 30- minute sessions at 10 hz. Thirty patients had sessions in Theta (5 hz) and experienced relaxation states of 50-100% after five minutes as well as improved pain relief. Eight patients had blood tests before and after the sessions and showed improved beta-endorphin levels of 10-50%. All of these relaxation results are improved when combining the photic stimulation with relaxation audio tapes.

Dr. Thomas Budzynski in "Biofeedback and the Twilight States of Consciousness," in G.E. Schwartz and D. Shapiro eds., Consciousness and Self-Regulation, vol. 1, New York, Plenum 1976 and non-published studies at the Biofeedback Institute of Denver, 1980:
Using a first-generation prototype, Dr. Budzynski concluded that "these devices produce a distinct relaxation state. Programming the device between 3 and 7 hz, it takes about 10 to 15 minutes for the patients to enter--effortlessly-a state of hypnosis. They terminate the sessions relaxed and with a feeling of well-being." Also, "the device has a calming effect on nervous or anxious patients. In a majority of cases the patients feel relaxed and calm during a period of three to four days after the session. It happens that the subjects have a reminiscence of childhood experiences, particularly when in Theta. They related their experiences which we incorporated into our psychotherapeutic program."

Dr. Gene W. Brockopp, Review of Research on Multi-Modal Sensory Stimulation with Clinical Implications and Research Proposals (non-published,1984):
Dr. Brockopp analyzed audio-visual brain stimulation and in particular hemispheric synchronization during EEG monitoring. "By inducing hemispheric coherence the machine can contribute to improved intellectual functioning of the brain. Like children spending most of their time in Theta, the machine allows a reduction in learning time. With adults a return into Theta allows them to rediscover childhood experiences. The machine is like a `lost and found office' for the subconscious."

Dr. Brockopp's conclusion is that dissipative structures allow the mind-via audio-visual stimulation- to abandon certain present neurological structures in order to maintain a higher, more coherent and flexible state of consciousness, thus allowing for improved communication of neuro-entities.

Dr. Norman Thomas and David Siever, University of Alberta, Florida. Several publications, notably: The Effect of Repetitive Audio/Visual Stimulation in Skeletomotor and Vasomotor Activity, 1989:

"We stimulated one of two groups of 30 people with a brain-stimulation device to test relaxation levels, using 10 hz frequency while observing their muscular tension with an EMG and their index skin temperature. The second group had to relax without machines via traditional means of autosuggestion. Most of the people in the second group said they felt relaxed while demonstrating greater tension (EMG) and lower skin temperatures, both of which are stress and nervous tension indicators. The group using the machine obtained deep relaxation state going beyond the programmed 15 minutes. EMG curves confirmed relaxation of the cortex due to the frequency adoption response."

These findings were also verified by James Greene and Dr. E.J. Baukus of FOCUS Human Research Development in Bourdonnais, Illinois. The muscular tension curve of the trapezius muscle were indicative of deep muscular relaxation.

Dr. Robert Cosgrove, Jr. of the anesthesia department of Stanford University School of Medicine, Stanford, California.

Dr. Cosgrove proceeded in 1988 with multiple experiences with the same devices and concluded that states of deep relaxation are obtained with these machines. "We are very optimistic about the possibilities of calming our patients before and after surgery. By the way, we already treat chronic stress affected patients. Thus, our EEG analysis shows that optimal cerebral functioning can be obtained with regular use of such audio-visual apparatus. The machines could eventually slow the decreasing cerebral performance with the elderly. This type of machine could 'revolutionize neurology and medicine.'"

Dale S. Foster of Memphis State University, "EEG and Subjective Correlates of Alpha Frequency Binaural Beats Stimulation Combined with Alpha Biofeedback," 1988:

Mr. Foster's conclusions indicate that the combination of binaural sounds with audio-visual stimulation machines allow access into Alpha states of consciousness much faster than with traditional biofeedback techniques.

Elisabeth Philipos, Pepperdine University, California, and James McGaugh, University of California, Irvine, have tested the effects of Theta frequencies on learning.

During their study a group of 20 students learned 1,800 words of Bulgarian in 120 hours while using Theta stimulation programs. In about 1/3 of normal time they spoke and wrote the new language.

D.J. Anderson, B.Sc., M.B., "The Treatment of Migraine with Variable Frequency Photo-Stimulation," in Headache, March 1989, pp 154-155:
D.J. Anderson used photo-stimulating goggles with variable frequency using red LEDs in order to stimulate the optic nerve, through closed eyes, right and left with frequencies between 0.5 and 50 hz. The study included seven patients who suffered a total of more than 50 migraines during the observation period. Forty-nine of these migraines were relieved (either by reducing the average duration or by increasing the frequency interval in between migraine crisis) and 36 other migraines could be stopped while using the goggles.

Dr. Glen D. Solomon, "Slow Wave Photic Stimulation in the Treatment of Headache-A Preliminary Report," in Headache, November 1985, pp 444-447:
Dr. Solomon works for the Department of Internal Medicine at the U.S. Air Force Medical Center in Scott, Illinois, where 24 patients with chronic headaches and migraines were treated with photic stimulation apparatus at 5-8 hz frequency. Fourteen of 15 patients with sustained headaches and 5 of 6 patients with chronic headaches noticed complete relief after the treatment. Four patients treated with the same photo-stimulation apparatus showed no reaction.

Bruce Harrah-Confort, Ph.D., Indiana University, "Alpha and Theta Response to the MindsEye Plus," 1990:
The study included 15 persons between the ages of 24 and 38 years old who were asked to relax via auto-suggestion with headphones dispensing a synthetic sound (100 cycles at 60 hz) and then to use the audio-visual stimulator MindsEye PlusTM. EEG graphic analysis showed that the first relaxation method did not alter the EEG-trace significantly vs. normal. MindsEye Plus users had, however, strongly improved Alpha and Theta tracings and experienced profound relaxation. There were also signs that would validate hemispheric synchronization during the experience.

Joseph Glickson, Department of Psychology, Tel Aviv University, "Photic Driving and Altered States of Consciousness: An Exploratory Study," in Imagination, Cognition and Personality, vol. 6(2), 1986-87, pp 167-182:
Four persons were exposed to photic stimulation in the 18, 10 and 6 hz ranges. A frequency response was established by two subjects during the initial session according to EEG measurements. These persons had an altered state of consciousness, and reported their visual and auditive experiences. The two other subjects had similar experiences during follow-on sessions. The study concludes that photic entrainment provokes altered states of consciousness according to the applied frequencies.

Paul Williams and Michael West, Department of Psychological Medicine, University Hospital of Wales and University of Wales Institute of Science and Technology, Cardiff, Wales, "EEG Responses to Photic Stimulation in Persons Experienced in Meditation," in Electroencephalography and Clinical Neurophysiology, 1975, 39, pp 519-522:
Williams and West tested photic entrainment on two test groups of 10 people. The test group produced significantly more Alpha waves and smaller Alpha blocking compared to the control group familiar with traditional meditation techniques. Alpha induction was realized faster and more frequently within the test vs. the control group.

Tsuyoshi Inouye, Noboru Sumitsuji and Kazuo Matsumoto, Department of Neuropsychiatry, Osaka University Medical School, Japan, "EEG Changes Induced by Light Stimuli Modulated with the Subject's Alpha Rhythm," in Electroencephalography and Clinical Neurophysiology, 1980, 49, pp 135-142:
Seven of nine persons undergoing the test obtained occipital Alpha of both hemispheres and concurrently coherence and phase between right and left occipital EEG. These results tend to confirm a hemispheric synchronization tendency by subjects using photic stimulation in the 10 hz (Alpha frequency) range.

Ronald Lesser, Hans Luders, G. Klem and Dudley Dinner, Department of Neurology, Cleveland Clinic Foundation, "Visual Potentials Evoked by Light- Emitting Diodes Mounted in Goggles," in Cleveland Clinic Quarterly, vol. 52, No. 2, Summer 1985, pp. 223-228:
A comparison of stimulation by strobiscopic lights and LED diodes shows that both methods have similar effects. LED stimulation may be preferable in intensive care units or during surgery because the type of stimulus is less disturbing.

Richard E. Townsend, Ph.D. of Neuropsychiatric Research, U.S. Naval Hospital in San Diego, "A Device for Generation and Presentation of Modulated Light Stimuli," in Electroencephalography and Clinical Neurophysiology, 1973, 34, pp 97-99:
The author describes a system allowing generation and presentation of modulated light stimuli with variable frequencies and wave forms. He concludes the possibilities of stimulation and positive responses during sleep-preparation and insomnia troubles.

Dr. William Harris, Director of the Penwell Foundation, USA in 1990:
Preliminary studies with audio-visual brain stimulators used by patients with AIDS indicate that "the devices are extremely efficient in terms of providing mental clarity, improved sleeping patterns (for sleep preparation and sleep duration) allowing for better physical disintoxication by the liver. The apparatus also stimulates immunology functions through states of deep relaxation."

Dr. Olivier Carreau, Saint-Louis Hospital in Paris, on "Efficiency of the MindsEye Plus audio-visual stimulator in treatment of the psoriasis during puvatherapy," study completed in January 1991.
Dr. Carreau analyzed 20 patients over a period of five months. Patients were treated one per week alternately via UVA and audio-visual stimulation (30-minute sessions) for psychosomatic skin disorders. All patients experienced deep relaxation during the sessions and had a feeling of well-being during the entire day. Five patients claimed that this feeling lasted for the following 2-3 days. Patients with combined therapy did better than with puvatherapy alone.

Transform Your iPod or any MP3 Player into a Portable Achievement Device

Find Out What You Can Achieve When You Dare to Relax!

ZenFrames + Your Brain = Success!

ZenFrames deliver gentle pulses of light and sound combined with guided visualization and soothing music to take you to the profound levels of relaxation known for focus, learning, achievement, and healing.

Want to lose weight? Just click on one of fifty-two titles, then relax and let your mind do the rest.

Is playing better golf your thing? Any of more than a dozen visualization sessions can easily help you master the game.

Maybe you just want a little time to get away from life's stresses. No problem. Simply choose a program from the stress-free series and enjoy a mental vacation.

A twenty-minute ZenFrames session can be equal to four hours of sleep. With hundreds of programs to choose from at ZenFrames.com, there's simply no limit to how good you can feel and what you can achieve.

If you want to get more done in less time, ZenFrames are for you!

Your ZenFrames comes with everything you need—you simply plug your ZenFrames into the earphone jack of your iPod or MP3 player and you're ready to dream big! Plus, when you register your ZenFrames, you get your own personal webpage for downloading new processes, tracking your progress and receiving updates. There's no software to install. You can take your portable achievement device with you wherever you go

Includes Six Bonus Visualization Sessions!

A $100 Value!

AM Focus
PM Dreamtime
AM Concentration
PM Release
AM Motivation
PM Success

Plus four music-only meditation sessions!

PorterVision's Product Resources

If You're Ready to Transform Your Life from the Inside Out, You've Come to the Right Place...

Four Mind Technologies in One Mind-Blowing Pair of Glasses!

Light Frequencies Distinctive flashing light patterns train your brain to operate in the best possible mode for creativity, focus, and mindfulness. If you are the type who likes to get things done, this form of brainwave entrainment can transform you into a mental powerhouse with the right mindset, energy and clarity to accomplish just about anything.

Binaural Beats Put simply, these are imbedded tones that the brain naturally follows into states of deep relaxation. Within minutes your brain reaches extraordinary levels of performance that would otherwise take years of practice to achieve.

Creative Visualization/Relaxation (CVR) CVR can help you change the way you view yourself and your life. Once you have a new image of yourself—as a healthy, happy, optimistic person—your fears and frustrations fade away and you no longer let small things stress you. CVR makes sure you are focusing on everything you want out of life so you can have it, effortlessly!

Mind-Music The music you hear on every PorterVision process is designed to create a full 360 degree experience that floods your mind with beautiful images and peaceful thoughts.
And so much more!

With CVR You'll Enjoy all these Benefits and More!

- The relaxation response replaces the fight-or-flight response.
- The right and left hemispheres of the brain become more balanced.
- Blood flow to the brain increases, resulting in clearer thinking, better concentration, improved memory, and enhanced creativity.
- Serotonin levels increase by up to 21 percent, calming the mind and body and creating an overall sense of well-being.*
- Endorphin levels increase by up to 25 percent, providing the brain with alertness, acting as a natural anti-depressant, providing relief from pain, and creating pleasurable and loving feelings.*
- Because 20 minutes on the ZenFrames can be like getting four hours of sleep, you'll find yourself sleeping less, feeling more rested, and accomplishing more.*
- Energy levels soar.
- Relationships become more fulfilling.
- Career satisfaction improves.
- A sense of purpose develops.
- The ability to make personal changes, such as losing weight, quitting smoking, ending nail biting or other nervous habits happens faster and easier.
- And last, but certainly not least, one gains a seemingly effortless ability to handle and manage stress.

Most people would pay thousands of dollars for a magic pill that offers these kinds of benefits. By using the ZenFrames, you see results in just a few relaxing minutes a day!
[
©2009 Zenframes is a trademark of PorterVision. iPod is a registered trademark of Apple, Inc.

PorterVision Books

Thrive in Overdrive, How to Navigate Your Overloaded Lifestyle
Patrick K. Porter, Ph.D.

In today's high-tech, fast-paced world, no one is immune to stress. Why? Because our lives are too overloaded. Thrive in Overdrive shows you how to rid yourself of the happiness-robbing condition called stress and enjoy a balanced life, but without giving up your overdrive lifestyle that makes sure you stay ahead of the game. The book, written by recognized how-to self-help expert, Dr. Patrick Porter, is based on methods that have been time-tested by over a million clients worldwide. He uses true stories, anecdotes, and deceivingly simple creative visualization exercises to demonstrate that, yes, you can have it all.

Awaken the Genius: Mind Technology for the 21st Century
Patrick K. Porter, Ph.D.

You'll discover how to maintain a Genuine positive attitude...how to unleash your personal passion and Enthusiasm (including stories and fun-to-do exercises)...how to develop Non-stop enrgy and center that energy on reaching your goals...how to activate your unlimited imagination and creativity...how to enjoy and unending drive to succeed...and...how to experience every day what geniuses throughout history have enjoyed-spontaneous intuitive breakthroughs.

Discover the Language of the Mind
Patrick K. Porter, Ph.D.

Discover the Language of the Mind, the Hypnotist's Guide to Psycho-Linguistics was previously published as Psycho-Linguistics, The Language of the Mind. This fully revised edition includes updates on dozens of new developments in the hypnosis field, full transcripts for each of the eleven processes, which includes two never-before published techniques as developed and tested by Dr. Patrick Porter and the experts at Positive Changes Hypnosis Centers. Psycho-Linguistics is a practical guide to the combined theories of hypnosis, Neuro-Linguistic Programming, Creative Visualization and Accelerated Learning - a perfect 'mind guide' for experienced hypnotists and psychotherapists or for anyone seeking a quick, easy, step-by-step method for self-improvement and enhanced communication.

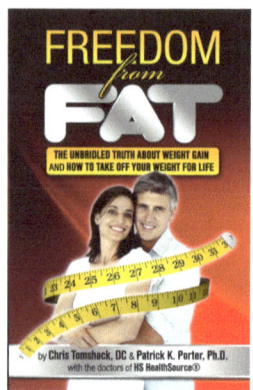

Freedom From Fat
The Unbridled Truth about Weight Gain and How to Take off Your Weight for Life

Patrick K Porter, Ph.D.
Chris Tomshack, DC
And the Doctctors at HealthSource® Chiropractctic

This is not another diet book! Rather, it's your chance to finally understand why you're gaining weight and how to reverse the cycle. By following the advice of these doctors, you can achieve safe, healthy and lasting weight loss success. If you're looking for a real world, step-by-step plan for taking off your weight and keeping it off, brought to you by doctors who are helping patients succeed even when all else has failed, this book is your answer.

Within these pages you will discover:

- *Why fad diets, gimmicks and complicated diet plans are doomed from the start*
- *The underlying condition that makes it nearly impossible for some people to lose weight, and how to fix it*
- *A system that addresses every part of the weight puzzle-diet, mental attitude, habits*
- *How to change the core causes of cravings, conditioned overeating, and weight gain so you can keep your weight off for life*

Six Secrets of G. E. N. I. U. S.
Patrick K. Porter, Ph.D.
Cynthia J. Porter, Ph.D.

Discover what inventors, artists and other great minds have known for centuries-the secrets of sparking their own creativity and super-charging their motivation. Learn simple strategies to rid yourself of negative thinking...to awaken your positive attitude in every situation...and to think your way through complex or confusing challenges. Discover what inventors, artists and other great minds have known for centuries-the secrets of sparking their own creativity and super-charging their motivation. Learn simple strategies to rid yourself of negative thinking...to awaken your positive attitude in every situation...and to think your way through complex or confusing challenges.

Weight Loss For Life in Ten Easy Steps
Todd Singelton, DC
Patrick K. Porter, Ph.D

If you could lose weight on your own, you wouldn't be holding this book in your hands right now. The experts all tell you to eat fewer calories and exercise more. If only it were that easy! The truth is, most people and most so-called experts have no idea what triggers the body to gain or lose weight. Few people recognize the clues (symptoms) that are your body's warning signals that your food choices aren't working. Add the fact that almost no one understands the relationship between stress and weight, and it's no wonder we have a nation of chronic dieters who stay overweight, unhealthy and unhappy no matter how hard they try. Well, today is your day...because you have in your hands the definitive guidebook for weight loss success that lasts. Within these pages we'll teach you everything you need to know to lose weight and keep it off for life, and it couldn't be simpler when all you have to do is follow ten easy steps! Together, we'll finally make your dream a reality so you can...

- Stop starving
- Be rid of cravings
- End emotional eating
- Turn off fat storage hormones
- Supercharge fat burning hormones
- Suppress your appetite naturally
- Clear up digestive problems
- Reverse the stress/weight effect
- Do away with habitual overeating
- Achieve radiant good health from the inside out!.

Welcome to The Gift of Love Project

The Gift of Love is a poetic writing that has its own beauty ... and upon further examination, it may lead one to a contemplative process, creating balance and harmony in one's everyday life. Over time, this process can also create subtle positive change in the recipient of **The Gift**.

My guidance leads me to distribute this writing to one billion people within the next two years. Hopefully, many people will be led to practice the contemplative process. If **The Gift of Love** resonates with you, please share it with others. As we gather and hold the **power of love** in our consciousness, we will dramatically reduce the level of anger, fear, and hatred on our planet today. -- Jerry DeShazo

The Gift of Love

I Agree Today
To Be The Gift of Love.

I Agree to Feel Deeply
Love for Others
Independent of Anything
They Are Expressing,
Saying, Doing, or Being.

I Agree to Allow Love
As I Know It
To Embrace My Whole Body
And Then to Just Send It
To Them Silently and Secretly.

I Agree to Feel it, Accept it, Breathe It
Into Every Cell of My Body on Each In-Breath
And On Each Out-Breath
Exhale Any Feeling Unlike Love.

I Will Repeat This Breathing Process Multiple Times
Until I Feel it Fully and Completely
Then Consciously Amplify In Me
The Feeling of Love and Project It to Others
As The Gift of Love.

This is My Secret Agreement –
No One Else Is To Know it.

This page may be reproduced in totality
for any peaceful purpose without financial gain.
All rights reserved, Jerome DeShazo, D.D., M.B.A.,M.C.C.

For more about The Gift of Love Project and to view the videos, please visit www.TheGiftofLove.com. You will also be given access to a special 9-minute Creative Visualization that will align you with the **Power of Love** and supercharge your day. Together we will change the world one person at a time.

http://www.thegiftoflove.com/

www.ingramcontent.com/pod-product-compliance
Lightning Source LLC
Chambersburg PA
CBHW041529220426
43671CB00002B/33